all
of
you

AMY RIORDAN

Dedication

For the women who feel crushed by the weight of sexual strongholds and the shame that comes with it.

I wrote this book for you.

I pray this is a tool that encourages you, challenges you, and gives you hope.

Most importantly, I pray it leads you closer to Jesus. He loves you, fully desires you, and wants *all of you*.

Contents

A Note to the Reader

I'm so glad you are reading this book. Whether you are approaching this with a hopeful heart or a guarded heart (or somewhere in-between), I am trusting the Holy Spirit will speak to you as you read this. As someone who has wrestled with sexual strongholds, I understand the secrecy, shame, and heavy weight that comes with it.

It is my prayer that you receive the hope, healing, and freedom you have been searching for.

If something in this book triggers you and you need a break, please take one. If something becomes too heavy, I encourage you to reach out to someone. I know this may sound impossible! I'll talk more about this later.

As time goes on, I may be publishing some additional material related to this book. I also hope to eventually have some online groups for women to go through this material together.

Please visit my website for more information or to sign up for my email newsletter.

I pray this book is a blessing to you!

Amy Riordan

longingforintimacy.com

Introduction

I spent many years of my life filtering what I shared with everyone, including God. I strived to show an acceptable side of myself to everyone around me while secretly feeling like there was something wrong with the way I was wired. I dealt with so much shame and had no idea how to tell anyone what I was wrestling with.

I felt incredibly alone.

I had great difficulty believing that Jesus didn't want me to filter what I shared with Him. I was afraid that He would be ashamed of me or angry when I attempted to finally be honest and transparent with Him about everything in my life including my hidden sexual sin. God slowly started showing me that He wanted all of me, not just what I saw as acceptable. He also started showing me it was safe to give all of myself to Him. This was not a trick to hold over my head or something He would use to shame me later.

If you are a woman wrestling with sexual strongholds, chances are you feel alone.

Even though this topic is rarely talked about within the church, many women are tied up by sexual strongholds. A stronghold is a mindset, value system, or thought process that hinders our growth in Christ. Strongholds, and the shame that accompanies them, are barriers that prevent our ability to know Jesus intimately.

Whether you are wrestling with pornography, masturbation, fantasies, sexual affairs, or lust toward men or women, this book is for you.

Do you love God yet find yourself entangled in sexual sin without knowing how to get out? I know it can feel completely paralyzing.

Sexual strongholds are often kept a secret because the weight of sexual sin carries so much guilt and shame. This separates us from God. He is the only one who can set you free. Do you know He wants all of you, not just the parts you feel safe and comfortable giving to Him?

He wants *all of you*.

What I share in this book is what I have found to be valuable in my own life and what I have shared with many other women over the past several years.

I am so thankful for the growing number of resources becoming available for women on this topic. We all have different perspectives, stories, expertise, and life experiences that make each resource unique. No matter where you are in your healing journey, I am praying this book is a tool to help your heart heal and for you to find freedom.

I also have a secret to share.

I have found throughout the years that what I learned in the process of breaking free from sexual strongholds has also been helpful in many other areas of my life. I had no idea that was going to be the case, but thankfully it is. This means what you learn in this book will also help equip you for other situations you may come across later.

I pray this book is a tool that encourages you, challenges you, and gives you hope. Most importantly, I pray it leads you closer to Jesus. He is the only one who can heal you, set you free, and satisfy your deepest desires.

1

My Story

I was one of those kids in the summertime who could easily be found on my back porch reading a book, fishing in the neighborhood pond with my friends, or walking to a nearby store to buy candy and a Teen Beat magazine. (That will give away my age, for sure.)

I'm so grateful to have had the kind of childhood where I can look back and have many fond memories. I was the wallflower child in school. My dad was a local elementary school teacher, and my teachers would often mention to me on the first day of school that they knew him. I always felt like everything I did would eventually get back to my parents somehow, so I did my best to blend in and not be noticed. The last thing I ever wanted to do was disappoint my parents.

I grew up going to church with my family every Sunday. I thought church was all about dressing up (which I hated) and doing the right thing. I learned all the books of the Bible in order, I knew many facts, but I did not know Jesus for myself. I didn't have a relationship with Him until many years later.

My parents were always very protective of me as I hit the dating years in high school. They always knew exactly where I was going, who I was going to be with, and I knew exactly when I had to be back home. Some boys did not like this, so they eventually broke up with me. Looking back, I can now see how that helped to weed out many boys I didn't need to be with in the first place. It certainly did not feel like that at the time, though.

I was raised to not have sex before marriage, and I never thought I would. I was pretty innocent and naïve during most of my teenage years. As I got older, my values became cloudy as I started putting more worth into being liked by boys.

Two months before I graduated high school, I did something I thought I would never do until I got married. I ended up having sex for the first time with a fairly new boyfriend. This experience left me wondering what all the hype was about concerning sex. I thought it was a terrible and confusing experience. It felt incredibly empty.

I quickly found out that he didn't care about me the same way I cared about him. I saw him in school after my accounting class the next school day, as I always did. This time he walked right past me with his friends. I was mortified, heartbroken, and so disappointed in myself.

Looking back, that experience opened the floodgate for me to participate in all kinds of things that I never considered doing before. It just didn't seem to matter anymore. I had already done what I thought I would never do before I got married, and I was feeling extremely disillusioned by it all.

That same year, I became very good friends with a girl I worked with. We quickly started spending a lot of time together outside of work. We had a deep connection that I had never experienced with anyone before. She understood me in a way no one else ever did. I felt like I had known her my whole life, even though I had known her just a short time.

I can still remember the two of us sitting in her car talking one day. I looked over to her and realized that I felt something I had never felt for another girl before. I felt an attraction to her that was different from what I experienced toward the boys I had dated over the years.

Around this same time, I was accidentally exposed to a graphic scene in a porn movie at someone's house. When this person turned on her TV, the movie started at a scene with several women on a bed together right before my unsuspecting eyes. They were doing things I had never even known existed before. While this person quickly panicked and turned off her TV, that scene etched itself into my mind and only increased the curiosity I was starting to experience.

Months went by, and my feelings for my friend grew as I started entertaining thoughts about her. I never challenged those thoughts. I wanted to be with her all the time. We eventually ended up in a physical relationship with each other, and this changed everything.

I didn't recognize it at the time, but I was trying to get from her what only God, Himself, could have given me. Something I had with her that I never had with any of the boys I dated was a sense of being fully known. She knew and accepted all of me. We were so incredibly dependent on each other that there wasn't much room for anyone else.

She eventually went her way, and I went mine. I didn't know what to do. She was my best friend and had become everything to me. My heart was absolutely shattered.

I had no idea how to move on, but I knew I had to.

To move on, I started dating a guy I worked with. Being with him opened up a whole new world to me that I had never been around before. We started drinking and using drugs together, and I eventually ended up watching porn with him. I wasn't interested in seeing the men at all, so I encouraged him to watch movies with two women in them. That became a very normal thing for us to do, and it seemed like harmless fun.

I didn't notice what was slowly happening. I was beginning to reprogram my mind to look at women differently. I started to see many more women in a sexual way. I was opening myself up to things that would affect me for many years to come. I just didn't realize it.

He and I eventually got married, but it didn't last long. I stopped using drugs and drinking right before we got married, but he didn't. I found out on our honeymoon that he drank more often than I had realized.

That was only the tip of the iceberg.

He went to the bar almost every night after work. There were times he didn't even know how he got home. One time I found him on the couch at night with extremely labored breathing. I can still remember what that sounded like. It was horrible. I was so worried about him that I almost called 911. I sat beside him all night long watching him breathe.

It wasn't until months later that he admitted to me that he was using heroin.

I, unfortunately, knew it was only a matter of time before we would be divorced. The weekend before our first anniversary, he moved out. He had always been one of the nicest guys I had ever met, but the drugs changed him so much. He was never anything but nice to me, but I felt like I didn't know him anymore.

I went back to church during that time because I was desperate to get my life back in order. I was 25 years old at that time and hadn't been to church in several years.

About six months after I started going back to church, God opened my eyes to show me how real He was, and I gave my life to Jesus. It was an amazing time in my life. Everything started to change rapidly. It was wonderful to learn that God had a plan for my life, and I didn't need to figure everything out on my own. I had a Bible from my first communion when I was younger, but I decided to buy a new one. I started taking in everything I could. The same Bible that was once just a boring book to me suddenly came alive.

Four months later, I received a visit from my former in-laws that will be forever etched in my heart. During their visit, they told me my ex-husband died of a heroin overdose two nights earlier. He had died on a Monday, and no one found him until Wednesday. My whole world, as I knew it, was turned upside down.

It was at that time that I learned one thing about God that I will never forget. Even when life seems so unsure, He never changes. He is always faithful.

After I gave my life to Christ, I started looking at my life so differently. I knew that if I was ever going to get married again, he would have to be a man who loved God with all his heart.

I soon met my current husband, Kevin, and we started dating right away. I loved his passion for God. Looking back, I really shouldn't have been dating anyone at that time. My heart needed to heal, but I jumped into another relationship like I had always done. I was carrying around an incredible amount of hurt, pain, and grief in my heart, and I did my best to shove it down. I didn't know what else to do.

Two years after we were married, I found myself dealing with postpartum depression after the birth of our first child. I struggled every day with feeling exhausted, overwhelmed, and I wanted to escape. I couldn't figure out why I couldn't get my life together, and it was months before I sought out help.

During this time, I started looking at lesbian porn online.

I knew I shouldn't do it. I did it anyway. I wanted to feel something other than emotional numbness. The porn evoked feelings in me that felt great at first, but I quickly realized I was in big trouble.

Unlike the other times I had looked at porn in the past, this time was different.

I didn't know how to stop.

I remember sitting in the kitchen at our former house thinking about how I could escape my life and start over. In all actuality, I had a great life. I had a wonderful husband and an adorable little boy who I loved so much. I was in complete deception in thinking I was living the wrong life.

The porn and fantasies I continually repeated in my mind completely rewired my brain. Lust had entered my heart and mind in a ravenous way.

I started to feel like I was looking at the world through a man's eyes and brain.

The day finally came when I confessed everything to my husband. I was concerned that if I waited one more day, I might never tell him. I had already tried to tell him several times. I felt such incredible shame, and I was terrified of what he would say or do. I didn't know how to make myself say it out loud, so I wrote my confession on a piece of paper and gave it to him when he came home.

He was devastated when he read that piece of paper, and I wasn't sure our marriage would ever heal. I had no idea what my next step would be, but I was so relieved to have finally told him.

After finally confessing all of this to him, I eventually stopped looking at porn after we set up accountability software that notified my husband of every website I visited. The thought of him seeing what I was searching for and had been looking at was a horrifying thought, so the fear mostly stopped me from continuing.

There were a couple of times I took the chance of looking at porn anyhow, because I figured he didn't always read his emails. I got caught both times, and I was mortified. I quickly discovered that having someone monitor my behavior didn't stop my thoughts from racing.

I was having horrible dreams that resembled the porn I used to watch, which made it all worse. I could battle these thoughts while I was awake, but as soon as I went to sleep, my imagination would go wherever it wanted.

The lust I felt just wouldn't go away. It affected all my friendships because I always stayed at arm's length from other women. I was so afraid that I might feel something I didn't want to feel. I felt like one person on the inside, but everyone else knew a different Amy on the outside.

I had no idea how often I fantasized about certain scenarios until I tried to stop. I didn't know how to stop obsessing about the thoughts I was having. I thought if I didn't give it all my attention, I would lose control in some way. That time of life, in many ways, was the most difficult part of my healing journey.

God has done so much in my life and my heart over the last few years, and I am not the same person I was. My marriage is also now stronger than it has ever been. God has healed us both in many ways.

I have been ministering to women who wrestle with sexual strongholds since 2010. Since the Holy Spirit started encouraging me to share my story, women all over the world have contacted me through my website to share their stories. God amazes me!

I once thought I was the only one. Maybe you have felt that way too.

Your path will look different than mine. If you're like me, this may be a book to go back to again later. God will show you something different as you progress in your healing.

So much of my life has been through a continued unraveling process. God will unravel everything, take out what doesn't belong, and then put everything back together again. I still have times when I feel the unraveling process starting again.

To be honest, I am in the middle of one of those times now. When I start to feel deep emptiness in the pit of my stomach that feels like it's going to swallow me up, I know God is working on my heart and is going to take me deeper with Him.

It's amazing to look back and see how much my heart has changed and how much I have found freedom over the past several years. God has been so faithful in continuing to heal my heart as

I yield everything over to Him. I believe He will do the same for you.

2

All of You

A few years ago, I walked past a sign in a store window that said, "Forever Desired." The words hit my heart immediately. Seeing that sign caused me to realize that a deep part of my heart craved being forever desired by someone.

I longed to be known by someone who wanted all of me. I believe we all have this longing deep inside of us. This is a longing to be desired by someone who not only knows the good and desirable parts of us, but also those parts we desperately try to keep hidden from everyone, including ourselves.

The older we get, the more unrealistic this can often seem. Heartbreaks, discouragement, and disappointments happen. Eventually, believing someone could wholeheartedly desire us forever can sound like nothing more than a fairy tale buried deep in our hearts.

I must confess that I have a goal in writing this book that extends much further than experiencing healing and freedom from sexual strongholds (although I am very excited about that part for you!). This book is filled with specific tools for you to be able to safely give all of yourself to the one who will ultimately set you free.

He wants all of you in the purest way possible.

He is the one who is closest to my heart. If you don't know Him intimately already, I am praying that you do by the end of this book.

I am referring to Jesus.

If you think being forever desired by Jesus as being equivalent to a cute saying written on a coffee mug, I assure you it goes much deeper than that. You were created to have a relationship with Jesus that is deeper than anything you could experience with anyone else on this earth.

You may be wondering why I am mentioning all of this in a book about breaking free from sexual strongholds.

I have found in my own personal life of finding healing and freedom, and in the lives of many women I have ministered to over the years, that sexual strongholds are not as much about sex as they are about a need for intimacy. This can be a bit shocking, and you may not believe me (yet). I didn't used to believe it either.

I had always equated sex and intimacy as being the same thing, but they are different.

When I was at one of my most desperate points of trying to break free from pornography and seemingly endless sexual fantasies, the Holy Spirit started showing me that what I was really craving was intimacy with Jesus.

I don't know about you, but I was a bit scared when I started learning about intimacy with Jesus.

I started to realize what a deep and unfulfilled need this was for me. I was afraid of my thoughts and honestly afraid of myself. I tended to sexualize many of the deep relationships I had. The last situation I wanted to find myself in was accidentally perverting my relationship with

Jesus. (That didn't happen, by the way, and I don't think it will for you either.)

Having an intimate relationship with Jesus means the deepest part of you is having a relationship with Him. It's about being vulnerable, loving, and trusting Him. It's about reading His Word and engaging in conversation with Him throughout your day. This is sharing the deepest parts of your heart with Him and listening for His voice and the Holy Spirit's guidance.

I am going to be giving you many tools in this book to help you start building intimacy with Jesus if you don't have this kind of relationship with Him already. Having this with Him is a huge key in breaking free (and staying free) from any kind of strongholds.

You see, Jesus wants all of you. He doesn't just want what you see as good, but He wants it all. The thought of this can be terrifying, even if it's something we know we need. It can feel like a huge risk letting someone know all of us inside and out.

There is an element of vulnerability involved here, for sure, and vulnerability involves trust. When sexual strongholds are involved, we often need to break free from layers of shame to help start building that trust with Him. I will be talking about breaking free from shame in Chapter 5.

"O Lord, you have searched me and known me! You know when I sit down and when I rise up; You discern my thoughts from afar" (Psalm 139:1-2).

God, the Father, not only created you, but He knows you fully inside and out. That can be a scary thought, especially if you are deeply entrenched in sin. That can be a sobering thought when you have repeatedly tried to change when it seems as if you have nothing to show for it at the end of the day.

He fully desires you and wants *all of you*.

"Jesus answered, "The most important is, Hear, O Israel: The Lord our God, the Lord is one. And you shall love the Lord your God with all your heart and with all your soul and with all your mind and with all your strength" (Mark 12:29-30).

He desires your whole heart, soul, mind, and all your strength.

Ironically, when we are trying to obtain healing and freedom, we can easily focus our whole heart, soul, mind, and strength on being set free.

What we need to do is shift all of this over to Jesus.

The healing and freedom you are wanting can only be found with His help and guidance. He already knows that you cannot do this on your own, or you would have done that by now. One of the most beautiful things you can have is an intimate relationship with Jesus.

I want to encourage you today. Jesus not only fully knows you, but He fully loves you. Jesus not only loves you, but He likes you. He doesn't just tolerate you. He knows it all, and He wants you.

All of you.

Reflection:

Do you strive to show only an acceptable side of yourself to others and God, not letting anyone truly know the real you?

Often, we don't just hide parts of our lives that are sinful, but we can also hide interests we have and hide God-given talents and traits that we think are small, silly, or will be misunderstood by others if we share them. What do you wish you could share with God and others that you have been keeping to yourself?

Action:

Read Psalm 139:1-6 out loud. Meditate on what this means for your own life:

"O LORD, you have searched me and known me!
You know when I sit down and when I rise up;
You discern my thoughts from afar.
You search out my path and my lying down
and are acquainted with all my ways.
Even before a word is on my tongue,
behold, O LORD, you know it altogether.
You hem me in, behind and before,
and lay your hand upon me.
Such knowledge is too wonderful for me;
it is high; I cannot attain it" (Psalm 139:1-6).

3

Where is Your Focus?

To find freedom, we can so often unintentionally cause ourselves so much extra discouragement and even despair that we were never meant to carry.

When we want to change something, we tend to put a lot of focus on it to find a solution. This is what I did when I continued to wrestle with sexual fantasies even long after I stopped watching porn. I discovered that I had a very difficult time not habitually fantasizing about certain scenarios that I had rehearsed in my mind for so long.

I decided that I needed to do whatever it took to get free. After all, I got myself into that mess, and I needed to get myself out of it. Right?

My solution was to pray more. I read the Bible more. I read more books. I researched blogs and websites. I obsessed about my sexuality and tried to pick everything apart. I put all my focus on making my temptations go away, but there was something I didn't know.

When we put all our focus on something, it also becomes the center of our view.

I had been putting all my focus on my temptations, so my temptations essentially became all I could see.

By praying all the time and continually pleading with God to change me, I thought I had been seeking Him because I was praying so much about it. It felt like the responsible thing to do. I started to realize that I had been approaching God for what He could do for me, instead of pursuing a deeper relationship with Him.

The Holy Spirit started showing me the importance of this scripture: "But seek first the kingdom of God and his righteousness, and all these things will be added to you" (Matthew 6:33).

I had been seeking healing and freedom first, not God.

If you have ever read anything else of mine or heard me speak, I am sure you may have heard me reference Matthew 6:33 at some point. It has become a life verse for me. Even years after breaking free from destructive patterns of sexual sin, this verse has remained invaluable to me.

Whatever we put our focus on grows.

We need to focus on Jesus, not what we are trying to overcome.

When we wrestle with sexual sin, it can often become something we either obsess about to overcome, or it can be something we attempt to completely ignore.

Maybe you are like me and worry if you don't put all your focus on changing, then you will go even deeper into sin. I didn't trust where I would go with all of it if I let go. I felt guilty and condemned myself for making such a mess of my marriage, so I decided to take complete ownership to fix it. While I did have the responsibility of seeking out healing for myself and our marriage, I put it all on myself instead of relying on God.

I was always trying to figure out how to fix myself. I did all of this in an honest effort to take responsibility for what I had done, but what I ended up doing was making it worse.

Have you ever done this?

There is, of course, nothing wrong with seeking help. I was praying and asking God to heal my heart all the time, so I didn't recognize that my focus was not in the right place. I felt like I was doing the right thing.

I thought putting all of my attention on how to stop fantasizing and looking at porn was pointing me in the direction of freedom. It was actually leading me into more bondage. There was no amount of obsessing or demeaning myself that could have healed my heart or set me free.

I only found freedom when I started taking the focus off of myself and putting my focus onto Jesus.

When we are trying to conquer sin or a particular stronghold in our lives, the Bible shows us to be guided by the Holy Spirit so we will not fall into sin.

"But I say, walk and live [habitually] in the [Holy] Spirit [responsive to and controlled and guided by the Spirit]; then you will certainly not gratify the cravings and desires of the flesh (of human nature without God)" (Galatians 5:16 AMP). I had this backwards for a very long time. Yes, we need to give God our best, but it doesn't work for long when we depend on our own efforts.

"For those who live according to the flesh set their minds on the things of the flesh, but those who live according to the Spirit set their minds on the things of the Spirit" (Romans 8:5).

We are to be led by the Holy Spirit.

If we are trying to overcome any craving or desire of the flesh, we need to be following and focusing our attention on the Holy Spirit. Otherwise, we will be trying to abstain from these cravings and desires in our own efforts. Our flesh will eventually rise up again in this area, and we need to be prepared to fight off the temptation and listen to the Holy Spirit as our guide.

God wants you to follow Him with your entire being. Continue pursuing Him. Lean on Him. Don't let shame and fear of failure get in between the relationship He wants to have with you. Seek the guidance of the Holy Spirit, and you will be able to conquer any stronghold with the grace He gives you.

Reflection:

Has your focus been on Jesus, or has it been on your temptations and how to quit sinning?

Maybe it's been on how disgusted you feel with yourself for not figuring out how to quit fantasizing or masturbating yet.

It can be very scary to shift your focus onto Jesus, but what you focus on becomes the center of your view. Putting your focus on Jesus (instead of your sin) is not the same as ignoring your sin. It's looking to the only one who can truly heal you and set you free.

Action:

Read Galatians 5:16 and Romans 8:5 again. What would it look like in your life if you applied these scriptures to the sexual strongholds you are wrestling with? I encourage you to pray and ask the Holy Spirit to give you wisdom concerning what it looks like to follow the Holy Spirit, so you do not gratify the sinful desires of your flesh.

This will require a shift in the way you are probably used to thinking. It may be incredibly uncomfortable. I am believing the Holy Spirit will show you how to change your thought patterns in this area. Once you get it, you can take it and run with it!

4

What Picture Do You Hold of Yourself?

I originally had this chapter placed toward the end of the book, but I decided to include it much earlier. How we see ourselves affects everything, including our healing process.

One day I was reading a devotional about the woman caught in the act of adultery in John 8, and a picture of her reaching up to Jesus was included. I felt an immediate connection to that picture. I related so much to what that picture was trying to convey. She was caught having sex with a man who was not her husband and was going to be stoned.

I could relate to all of it. I was never caught in the physical act of being intimate with anyone, but I had been incredibly unfaithful to my husband and God with pornography, masturbation, and the fantasies that constantly circled through my mind. I could have easily been caught. Thankfully I confessed everything to my husband before I was.

I had dealt with shame and sin in my life that enabled me to look at that image of scripture and be able to see myself. I think many of us could.

While looking at that picture, the Holy Spirit spoke something so clearly to my heart.

He said, *"That is not who you are."*

I was confused for a bit as to why He would point that out to me. As the days went by, I started to realize, even years after finding so much freedom in my life, I still saw myself as the woman who was about to be stoned. It wasn't a past tense scenario for me. It was still present tense.

I had never updated the picture my heart carried around of myself. I may have found freedom from many unwanted sexual behaviors, but I left my mind unrenewed regarding how I saw myself.

How we see ourselves affects everything. It affects how we act, what we think, what we say, how we carry ourselves, the decisions we make, and how we live our lives. The view we have of ourselves affects how determined or driven we are, how passive or controlling we are, and how we treat others.

Even long after I broke free from sexual strongholds, I started to see that the mental image I had of myself was the same as it used to be. I still saw myself as this sinful woman about to be stoned, except I felt as though I was on my best behavior.

That is only a behavior change, not a heart change. God has done so much more than that! Jesus has healed my heart and set me free, and He continues to do so. This is much more than being on my best behavior.

No matter what part of the healing journey you are on concerning sexual wholeness, the way you see yourself is so important. If you see yourself as sinful and broken, you will act that way. I am not saying that we need to lie to ourselves, but our view of ourselves is powerful. How we see ourselves affects our actions.

How do you see yourself?

It took seeing and connecting to that picture to realize I needed to change the mental image I had of myself.

How often do we stay stuck due to a picture we hold of ourselves that has never been renewed?

To embrace the people God created us to be, we must see ourselves as Jesus does. Our actions follow our thoughts and heart posture. If you have given your life to Christ and you are letting Him change you from the inside out, you are not who you used to be.

If you see yourself as broken and dirty, this is not how Jesus sees you.

This also helps tremendously with temptations because they will most definitely come your way. If you see yourself the way Jesus sees you, the temptations will be easier to resist. It won't feel like who you are anymore.

You need to see yourself as the woman you are becoming in Christ. This will help propel you into the destiny He has for you, and it will also propel you into deeper healing in your heart.

What does the mental picture I hold of myself look like now? I no longer identify as the woman ready to be stoned. My past has been redeemed in so many ways. An accurate picture would be a woman who knows intimacy with Jesus, whose heart has been healed, who has had many layers of shame melt off of her, and a woman who knows how much she is loved by her Creator.

Isn't it amazing what Jesus can do with a life surrendered to Him?

Reflection:

What is the mental picture you have of yourself? Does it match the one God has of you? Does it consist of defeat or hope?

Have you had any harmful (on purpose or not) words spoken over you by someone that you took to heart? This can affect you deeply because your actions follow your thoughts and the posture of your heart.

Do you continually speak words over yourself that are harmful? We can easily do this when we feel defeated and are so tired of our sin, but this hurts our hearts. It doesn't motivate us to change. When you believe lies about yourself, you are less likely to fight against temptation in that area.

Let me write that last sentence again: *When you believe lies about yourself, you are less likely to fight against temptation in that area.*

Action:

Search out God's Word to find what He has to say about you. Write a statement with affirmations from the Bible about who you are in Christ and make it specific to what you are dealing with.

Read it out loud to yourself. Stop and think about what you are saying. Put it on your bathroom mirror, phone, or where you can see it and read it every day until your mind is renewed in this area. Even if you have done this before, I encourage you to do it again. It can take a while to renew your mind when you are so used to thinking another way.

5

Breaking Free from Shame

A key component to breaking free from sexual strongholds is identifying and breaking free from shame. This is done layer by layer.

Many years went by before I started to realize how much shame was affecting the way I saw myself, so many of my decisions, my relationships with others, not to mention my relationship with God.

Shame is different from guilt. Guilt says, "I *did* something bad." Shame says, "I *am* bad."

Shame wants to stay hidden. It becomes attached to our identity, which is why I think it can be so difficult to recognize sometimes. Some of us have carried shame around with us for practically our entire lives, so we have never known any differently.

I kept my struggles with pornography, lust, and sexual fantasies all to myself because I was sure I was the only Christian woman dealing with such a thing. When I did finally find a resource that helped me, I felt such shame because it was written for men. The articles talked about lusting after women (which is exactly what I was doing) so most of it was relatable to me. I already felt like I was dealing with a man's issue, so this only solidified my fears that I was defective as a woman.

Most women, no matter the kind of porn they are viewing, fear they are wrestling with a man's issue. This is not true. Men are not the only ones who are visually wired.

When I did finally find an online forum for women struggling with pornography, I was incredibly triggered by the discussion. I quickly discovered that being in a group with women talking about masturbation was not the place for me to be. I felt even more shame thinking I was different than all the other women who wrestled with porn.

If you are wrestling with porn, no matter what kind it is, shame will do its best to keep you trapped. Many women struggle with sexual sin of all kinds, but it is unfortunately still not talked about in the church as often as it needs to be. This can lead us (and others) to believe women just don't wrestle with sexual strongholds. This is not true.

Whether you are struggling with porn, sexual fantasies, masturbation, or lust toward men or women, Jesus wants all of you. You are not alone, and Jesus can set you free.

Shame can affect just about every area of our lives, including our relationships. Shame affects:

- How we see ourselves: "There is something wrong with the core of who I am."
- Our relationships with others: "I could never let anyone find out who I really am."
- Our relationship with God: "God must hate me. I can't approach Him until I am over this."

In Genesis 2:25, God created Adam and Eve, "And the man and his wife were both naked and were not ashamed." It wasn't until Genesis 3:6-10, when Eve took the fruit, ate it, and gave some to Adam, that their eyes were opened, and shame entered the picture:

"So when the woman saw that the tree was good for food, and that it was a delight to the eyes, and that the tree was to be desired to make one wise, she took of its fruit and ate, and she also gave some to her husband who was with her, and he ate. Then the eyes of both were opened, and they knew that they were naked. And they sewed fig leaves together and made themselves loincloths.

"And they heard the sound of the Lord God walking in the garden in the cool of the day, and the man and his wife hid themselves from the presence of the Lord God among the trees of the garden. But the Lord God called to the man and said to him, 'Where are you?' And he said, 'I heard the sound of you in the garden, and I was afraid, because I was naked, and I hid myself.'"

When we hide from God due to our sin or shame, the hold it has on us just keeps growing. We can recognize shame by examining the thoughts that go through our minds, such as:

- I am the only woman who deals with this. I could never tell anyone.

- I need to hide this. This must just be who I am.

- There is something wrong with the core of who I am.

- I caused that person to abuse me. Part of it felt good. It was my fault.

- I am defective as a woman.

- I am disgusting.

These are some additional indicators of shame:

- Feeling incapable of doing anything, trapped by invisible walls all around you

- Being performance-driven

- Beating yourself up for even the slightest mistakes

- Letting people abuse you or treat you horribly because you don't feel you deserve better

- Keeping relationships surfacy (including your relationship with God)

- Struggling with strongholds secretly

- Feeling buried in what you have done (or keep doing)

Shame is a barrier to building intimacy with Jesus and building close, healthy relationships with other people. We cannot have a close relationship with someone we are hiding from.

Jesus can remove these layers of shame from you. He can remove the shame that is preventing healing, and He can remove the shame that keeps you going back for more of what you promised yourself you would stop doing a long time ago. Jesus can also remove the shame that prevents you from seeing yourself the way God does.

Psalm 139:14 says, "I praise you, for I am fearfully and wonderfully made. Wonderful are your works; my soul knows it very well."

If you are buried in shame, it can be very difficult to truly believe that you are fearfully and wonderfully made. Instead, shame will cause you to believe there is something wrong with the core of who you are.

Zephaniah 3:17 says, "The LORD your God is in your midst, a mighty one who will save; he will rejoice over you with gladness; he will quiet you by his love; he will exult over you with loud singing."

Have you started seeing some of the ways shame has been affecting you?

It is safe to reveal your heart to Jesus. He doesn't shame us like people can, or like we can shame ourselves. Coming out of hiding and into His presence with our sin and brokenness can be scary, but I promise you He will never shame you. He won't back away from you or be overwhelmed with what you will tell Him. He isn't disgusted by you either.

He wants to repair and heal your heart. It might feel like it's too late. That is a lie from the pit of hell. Jesus wants your heart. He wants all of you.

Reflection:

What are some of the ways shame has been affecting you?

Have you been able to recognize the lies shame has spoken to you? What does God say about you instead?

Action:

Once you become aware of the ways shame speaks to you, it will take diligence to rebuke and reject those thoughts when they come. Shame can sound like your own voice. "I'm worthless. I'm so disgusting." but that's the voice of shame. This is a process that takes diligence because we often don't realize how often shame can try to hinder us. There is incredible freedom on the other side!

Pray that the Holy Spirit will show you when you are believing or rehearsing a lie that shame has been telling you. Practice rebuking that thought right away and speaking God's Word over yourself instead.

If you wrote down affirmations from the last chapter about who you are in Christ, this will also be helpful when battling shame.

6

Reaching Out

I resisted talking to anyone about my sexual sin and temptations for years. I felt such incredible shame and was afraid I would scare someone away if I was completely honest about what I had been doing and the kind of thoughts that went through my mind daily.

No one had the slightest idea that I had been dealing with a porn addiction, and I didn't want to see the shock or disappointment on their faces when I told them. I was the last person they would have suspected, as is often the case.

A few years after confessing everything to my husband, I finally reached out to a woman from my church who was a Christian counselor. I wish I wouldn't have waited so long. I hadn't been looking at porn anymore, but the thoughts and fantasies continued to race through my mind. Processing everything out loud with someone other than my husband helped me so much.

"Therefore confess your sins to each other and pray for each other so that you may be healed. The prayer of a righteous person is powerful and effective" (James 5:16 NIV).

Have you reached out to someone for counsel, wisdom, and prayer? I know it is not easy. (That is an understatement.)

If you share just a little bit of your story with someone you can trust, you will know by her reaction if she is a good person for you to continue reaching out to.

I often encourage women to test the waters by sharing a little bit of their story with someone first instead of sharing their entire heart and life history all at once with someone they are turning to for wisdom or counsel. There are two reasons for this. First, some people do not know how to handle other people's pain. They are not equipped for it. There are many reasons for this, but it is valuable information to have when reaching out to someone.

Maybe you tried to talk to someone before and it didn't go very well. I am so sorry if that happened to you. Taking a huge risk in talking to someone and it not going well can be so incredibly painful. I have been there, and I understand. I encourage you to take a deep breath (or many deep breaths) and pray about another person you might be able to reach out to.

I have found that sometimes even the most well-meaning people honestly don't know what to say or do when a woman confesses sexual temptations to them. They can unintentionally say something insensitive, or (out of not knowing how to respond) say nothing. Either reaction can feel like an incredible sting of rejection.

Second, sexual strongholds and the weight of history that can go along with it, can be very heavy. After keeping everything to yourself for so long, there can be a desire to tell someone your entire life story once you get started. It's like opening a valve and before you know it there is a flood. That's an incredibly heavy weight for someone to hold. While you might feel better after, that is very difficult for a person to process.

You know this well because you feel the weight of it every day. Maybe you've carried the weight of this burden so long that you don't know what it feels like without it. I'm believing that someday, with Jesus' help, you will.

For this reason, it can be helpful to write down ahead of time some ideas of what you could share with someone. You wouldn't have to stick with it, but it might help give you direction if you get stuck and don't know what to say. It can also help you stay focused without going into too much all at once.

You do not have to find someone who has wrestled with sexual strongholds of her own. That would be helpful, but it is not at all necessary. The person who helped me the most had not struggled in the same ways I did, but I knew she was a strong and compassionate Christian, and she always pointed me to Jesus. She had also overcome some very challenging experiences in her own life that she was transparent with others about. This encouraged me because I knew she wasn't a stranger to working through painful experiences.

I recommend talking to another woman rather than a man due to the kind of details you will share. For those of you who are married, it is often beneficial to reach out to someone trustworthy in addition to your spouse. My husband and I agreed for me to tell him when I was feeling tempted so we could pray. This was not easy for us to do, though. Each couple needs to decide what works best for them.

For those who read this who experience same-sex attraction, something that was helpful for me was finding someone older than me to talk to. The counselor from my church whom I mentioned earlier was around my mom's age. I felt safer sharing intimate details of my life with her because I knew I would never be attracted to her.

Having someone who can encourage you and steer you in the right direction when you feel overwhelmed is invaluable. I wish I wouldn't have waited as long as I did to reach out to someone. If you are reading this and do not have someone in your life to talk to, I am praying that you seek God for someone wise and trustworthy you can confide in. It is so important.

Reflection:

Have you found someone to reach out to regarding the temptations and unwanted sexual behaviors you have been wrestling with?

Action:

Read James 5:16 again. How does this scripture apply to reaching out to someone for prayer and guidance? If you have not been talking to someone about this, what would be the downfall for continuing to not reach out to someone? What could be the benefits of taking the chance to reach out?

7

Knowing the Heart Healer

Many of us walk around with wounds in our souls that stem from any number of circumstances that happen in our lives. We have wounds that need to be treated, but they are often hard to see because they are on the inside. The effects of a wounded soul can show up in significant ways.

Many of us shove down the pain we feel. Others of us may explode in anger when a wound is touched. We try to deal with what we see (the anger, frustration, etc.), but these are symptoms of the wound, not the actual wound itself. Sometimes we can carry the weight of things for so long that we don't even recognize how much we're carrying anymore.

I used to think that the sexual strongholds in my life were my biggest problem.

When Jesus started healing my heart, He gently started showing me how much pride I was dealing with. He gently started showing me that I didn't trust Him or His will for my life. I lived in so much unbelief. He also gently started showing me that I was holding onto unforgiveness toward many people. I'll talk more about that in the next chapter.

He started healing deep wounds I had from many different situations that had accumulated over the years.

When our souls are restored, it is so much easier to rise above everything that has been weighing us down.

Jesus knows your heart even better than you do, and He wants to heal you and make you whole. He does not run away from brokenhearted people. He stays near to us.

We can say that He is for us, but do we truly know this?

Psalm 34:18 says, "The Lord is near to the brokenhearted and saves the crushed in spirit."

The Amplified Classic Version says, "The Lord is close to those who are of a broken heart and saves such as are crushed with sorrow for sin and are humbly and thoroughly penitent."

Penitent means "to feel or to express remorse."

This adds something completely different from what I thought crushed in spirit meant. The Lord is not only close to the brokenhearted, but He saves those who are crushed with sorrow for their sin.

Are you brokenhearted? Are you crushed in sorrow for your sin?

God has not distanced Himself from you. Instead, He remains close.

Jesus heals broken hearts. He is near you and hasn't turned His back on you. He isn't ashamed of you. He wants you to give all of yourself to Him, not just the pretty parts. He loves you.

It can be terrifying to even think about dealing with the pain hidden deeply in your heart, but you need to know that the safest place your heart can be is with the Lord.

Maybe you struggle with shame due to something that happened to you against your will. The Lord saw what happened, and you are not to blame. He loves you and knows the depths of your heart. He doesn't see you the way you see yourself. He sees someone who is beautiful and pure. He sees you as He created you to be, and this is your true identity.

You can trust your heart with Him.

Have you been able to be transparent with God? I encourage you to meditate on Psalm 34:18. When we know He is truly with us when we are remorseful for our sin, it is so much easier to fully give our hearts to Him and be transparent with Him.

We can also wrestle with incredible regret. Many of us carry around regrets that affect us much more than we may realize. The weight of sexual sin and the damage it causes can be very heavy. The weight of what led up to the sexual sin is heavy too. When we try to stop unwanted sexual behaviors repeatedly, only to do the same thing a few days later (or later the same day), it can start to numb our hearts. It damages our hearts, our relationships with others, and it damages our relationship with God.

This is partly why I talk so much about building intimacy with Jesus. It's difficult to embrace the intimacy and joy we can have with Him when we are weighed down with regret.

We have an enemy who loves to lie to us. He loves to tell us, "You cannot trust anyone! You will always deal with this! There is something horribly wrong with you! You are going to live like this forever. God is disgusted with you."

This is not true though. Jesus wants to heal your heart so you can embrace the hope and joy He has for you. Then you can walk in an intimate relationship with Him and effectively do what He's called you to do.

He has so much more for you than living life with a numb or heavy heart, just existing, or stressed out all the time.

Jesus can heal you. It is not too late. Jesus can heal any wound, no matter how big or small or how long ago it happened. He can also heal your brain. He did this for me, and He can do this for you. God will forgive you if you ask Him with all sincerity to forgive you. It is not too late to repent (turn) from your sin. He will give you the grace you need to do this.

If you have never given your life to Him, or maybe you have started to walk away, you have an excellent opportunity to give your life to Him right now. Being set free from sexual strongholds and having your heart healed is amazing, but there is something even better and more important that He wants you to have. He not only wants to be your heart healer and restorer, but He wants to be your Lord and Savior.

He paid for all your sins by dying on the cross for you. I can assure you that I would not have made it this far without Him being my Lord and Savior, and I wouldn't want to live life any other way. He has saved my life in more than one way.

I want to encourage you that Jesus can restore you. He can heal you and save you. It is absolutely not too late. He can make new what has been broken. He can even give you what you may not ever remember having before. He loves you and is fighting for you.

Reflection:

When we're dealing with anger, frustration, and grief, etc. we are seeing the symptoms of a wound, not the actual wound itself. What are some symptoms you have been dealing with?

Action:

Do you believe Jesus can heal the wounds in your heart? I encourage you to pray and ask Jesus to heal you. The wounds go deeper than the symptoms you see. Jesus desires to heal and restore you.

If you have never given your life to Him or have walked away, ask Him to forgive you for your sins and He will. Ask Him to save you and lead you and guide you by becoming your Lord and Savior. Say this as a prayer out loud to Him. There are no right or wrong words to use. He is looking for a sincere heart, not an elegant prayer.

8

Victory Over
Anger & Unforgiveness

When Jesus started setting me free from the strongholds in my life, He started showing me how much unforgiveness and anger I had in my heart. I never gave much thought to it, until God started showing me what was in my heart and how it was affecting my life in drastic ways. I was holding onto so much unforgiveness against many people (including myself), and I honestly had no idea until the Holy Spirit started showing me what my heart looked like.

Left unchecked, unforgiveness will eventually turn into bitterness and can affect us for quite some time before we realize what it's doing to us physically, emotionally, and mentally.

You may wonder what anger and unforgiveness have to do with breaking free from sexual strongholds. Many times, when Jesus starts healing our hearts in certain areas, it clears the way for other areas to be healed.

I want to pause right here to acknowledge that many of you have had some horrific things happen to you. I am so very sorry for what you have been through. I am not at all suggesting that what happened to you is okay. Forgiving others is not the same thing as saying what someone did is okay.

If someone purposefully cut my arm and it caused an open wound, I could choose to forgive them, but my arm would still hurt terribly until it eventually healed. Unforgiveness is like an infection. My arm would not heal if it had an infection. The infection would have to be removed first. I would need to forgive that person (remove the infection) because God has commanded me to forgive. This isn't because He doesn't care, but He knows the infection would remain otherwise. Once the infection was removed, my arm could start to heal. This is all a process.

When God tells us to forgive others, this is not the same as Him telling us to "get over it." Forgiveness is when we choose to release the situation to God. Otherwise, He knows that bitterness will start to take root in our hearts. Forgiveness is for your benefit. It allows God to deal with the situation and gives Jesus the opportunity to heal our hearts.

Many of us have been bitter, and we don't even recognize it. This is scary to think about. This can cause us to be unable to live in the present, and we can also find ourselves living in the past. Unforgiveness piling up in our hearts can leave us with a wounded, numb, and hard heart.

As I mentioned in the previous chapter, when Jesus started healing my heart, anger was one of the first things to rise to the surface of my heart.

It didn't just rise to the surface either. It started overflowing everywhere.

When Jesus started showing me what my heart looked like in this area, I didn't know what was going on. Everything was making me angry. Everything and everyone offended me. I was constantly angry with my husband. I would explode over nothing.

I didn't realize God was at work.

He was drawing out and exposing what had been deeply buried in my heart.

One by one I started making detailed lists of people I needed to forgive. Some situations on my list were recent, others were many years old. I had been storing all of it up, and a root of bitterness was forming in my heart.

"See to it that no one fails to obtain the grace of God; that no 'root of bitterness' causes trouble, and by it many become defiled" (Hebrews 12:15).

It was during this time that I started to realize God was up to something.

He was beginning to heal my heart.

This was a bittersweet time in my life. God was exposing so much in my heart that I didn't know was there. My emotions felt raw, and I was beginning to have many memories from the past come back to my mind. I thought it was the enemy at first, but then I realized it was God healing my heart.

He was bringing these situations back up again, one by one, to heal my heart. Many of those situations had happened years prior, but they were still affecting me.

Sometimes we don't realize how much we have held onto until it starts rising to the surface of our hearts. We can hold so much against ourselves, even with situations that we asked God to forgive us for years earlier.

When we have unwanted sexual behaviors that we have been wrestling with for a long time, we can become angry with ourselves. I probably don't have to tell you that. This anger only compounds the problem, and we can end up condemning ourselves so much that we give up. Self-hatred can even settle in. Does this sound familiar?

If it wouldn't be effective to talk to someone else so harshly, we shouldn't speak to ourselves this way either. It all backfires. We can often be much harder on ourselves than anyone else.

Have you been dealing with anger that keeps coming up to the surface frequently? Maybe you are angry about a situation that happened recently or one that happened a while ago. Either way, God wants you to make the decision to forgive so He can remove the infection and heal your heart.

Reflection:

Is there someone you need to forgive?

You can pray and ask the Lord to reveal anyone whom you need to forgive. Write down any person or situation that comes to mind. Take your time and know that you don't need to dig anything up. The Holy Spirit will remind you of whom you need to forgive. You may cry when going through this list. It's okay to cry! Jesus heals through tears.

Action:

*If this next part is particularly difficult for you, please do not hesitate to ask a counselor, pastor, or mature Christian friend to accompany you as you do this. They will be able to pray for you and support you. I have found this to be very helpful along the way.

After you write down your list of people, this is an example of a confession you can say out loud for each person:

"Lord, I choose to forgive _____ for _____ even though it made me feel _____."

This is a sample prayer you can say afterward:

"Lord, I choose to not hold on to resentment. I choose to release every offense and trauma named. I repent for every sin I committed as a result of these offenses. I thank You, Lord, that as I release them, I am being released.

"Lord, I now ask You to come and heal my damaged emotions. I ask that You bind up my broken heart and heal every wound that was inflicted by hurtful words, emotional, sexual, physical, and spiritual abuse. I open my heart to You and ask You to come and do a deep work in me. Lord, I ask that You heal my heart. In Jesus' name, I pray. Amen"

9

When Temptation Comes

Many years went by where I felt incredible guilt and condemnation over being tempted by something I saw, or even by a thought that would suddenly pop into my head. I would immediately feel guilty, ashamed, and very critical of myself, so it was even more difficult to resist the temptation.

Jesus lived a sinless life here on earth and He was tempted. That's how we can know it's not a sin to be tempted. If Jesus was tempted, we are going to be tempted also. It's what we do with that temptation that matters greatly.

Do you know what triggers you? To avoid falling into the same trap repeatedly, we need to know our triggers. I can guarantee you that the devil knows our triggers.

We need to be mindful of the movies we watch, books we read, what we look at on social media, conversations we take part in, etc. How do you feel afterward? Are you friends with people (including people you once dated) on social media that trigger you to fantasize about sexual scenarios with them? Are you believing any lies about yourself, others, or God that are triggering temptations for you?

Sexual sin can most definitely have an element of familiarity and comfort that comes along with it. This can make it so much more challenging to let go. If there is something sinful in your life that causes you continual temptation, find a way to cut it out. Don't just try to be stronger next time. Some activities are sinful and need to be cut out forever. Other activities may be triggers right now but might not be a trigger forever.

Are you believing any lies about yourself, others, or God? When we are believing lies about ourselves, others, or God, the decisions we make can often reflect those same lies buried in our hearts and minds. This can fuel temptations. They can help serve as our justification in the moment to look at porn, fantasize, or masturbate.

As Jesus continued to gradually heal my heart, the Holy Spirit started revealing to me lies I had been believing about myself, other women, and my husband. I started to see how these lies worked to add fuel to many of the temptations I continued to deal with.

One of the lies I believed is that men could never be trusted. Without realizing it, this helped me to justify watching lesbian porn. It also fueled temptations for me when my husband and I got into arguments, when he did something that emotionally hurt me, or when he was gone for an extended period of time.

If you pray and ask the Holy Spirit to reveal to you any lies you have been believing, I am trusting He will show you. You don't need to go digging for this (please don't do that to yourself). He will show you when the time is right.

Some days you may feel more vulnerable. We all have those days. These are days when we are tired, stressed, bored, just before or during our period, and difficult days in general. During times like this, it would be incredibly helpful to pray right away (as soon as you realize it may be a challenging day) so you can equip yourself for the day to come.

"No temptation has seized you except what is common to man. And God is faithful; He will not let you be tempted beyond what you can bear. But when you are tempted, He will also provide a way out so that you can stand up under it" (1 Cor. 10:13).

God tells us that there is always a way out of situations that tempt us. It is not impossible to fight it even though it may feel almost next to it at times.

As far as masturbation goes, when are you most susceptible? Is it when you're stressed or lonely? Bored? Before you go to sleep at night? Do you see a pattern?

When you see that pattern, ask God to fill that specific need in your life. If it's when you are feeling stressed, bored, sad, or lonely, for example, you can ask Him to come into the situation and help you. If it's before you go to sleep at night, ask Him to help you form a new routine before you go to bed.

Stop what you are doing and ask Him out loud to help you. Yes, this will be the last thing you will feel like doing in the moment. That is why you need to do it. Asking the Holy Spirit out loud to step into the situation to help you when you are tempted to masturbate can be very difficult. It is very effective though.

There are so many simple things we can do when we're facing temptation. The problem is it's just as easy not to do them. We must choose to do them. This can be as simple as leaving the room, going outside if possible, or calling someone. Focus on your other senses by stopping to look around the room and taking note of what you see. Do you hear anything outside? Even just focusing on that can help change your thought process.

Something that has helped others that may be helpful for you is to write in a notebook (or on your phone, etc.) some ideas of what you can do when you are tempted to look at porn, fantasize, read things you know you shouldn't read, or masturbate. Be specific.

You will want this to be something you can keep private but access easily and quickly. Maybe you can put a scripture in there that has been helpful for you in the past, an activity that helped you change your focus, or a person you could talk to as a distraction.

Think back to what has worked for you in the past. Is there something the Holy Spirit spoke to your heart once that helped you? Write it down.

Include words of encouragement to yourself of how far you've come over time. This sounds oversimplified, perhaps, but it can be more powerful than it sounds. When you have it all in front of you when temptation hits, it can be very helpful. Then you are not searching for something to help you when you're in the moment later on.

As time goes on you may not need this, but it is good to have, especially during more vulnerable times. Something that has worked for me is saying out loud, "Jesus, please fill this place in me that is wanting something else right now. I am making the decision to choose You."

Use times of temptation to practice being transparent with Jesus.

When I was finally in a place where I felt like I could be transparent with God about my struggles, layers of shame started falling off me one by one. I was still finding myself tempted by thoughts of other women, but something started to change.

As I continued to seek Him first and continued to build intimacy and transparency with Jesus, the temptations I had were not as strong anymore. Little by little, I was finally able to specifically say *out loud* to God:

"I am really struggling with the temptation to look at porn right now. Please help me."

"I have been thinking lustful thoughts about someone again. Please forgive me. I give my deep need for intimacy to You and ask You to fill this place in me again."

This is when I realized He wanted me to talk to Him about the temptations and longings I faced.

Remember, He wants all of you. He already knows what tempts you. He wants you to come to Him during these times. It can feel very awkward and embarrassing, but I encourage you to say all of this out loud to Him, as well. It is extra powerful when we can hear ourselves say this out loud. Eventually, your brain and heart will start to default to Jesus when you keep your focus on Him.

Reflection:

Do you recognize a pattern of when you seem to be most vulnerable to temptation? Do you have a plan in place for when temptation hits?

Action:

The next time temptation comes your way, practice confessing what you are dealing with (out loud) to God. Be specific. This will help you build transparency and intimacy with Him. This becomes easier as time goes on. As you become more comfortable confessing temptations to Him, practice turning to Him even quicker than you did before. The quicker we confess temptation, the less power it will have.

10

What Does Healing & Freedom Look Like?

If you were within walking distance of a place you wanted to visit, it would be very challenging to get there if you didn't know which direction to go, what street it was on, or what landmarks to look for nearby.

This is how it can feel to want healing from sexual strongholds if we don't know how to get there or even what it's supposed to look like when we arrive.

I was hoping and praying for the day when I would wake up and all my temptations would be gone. The truth is healing and freedom is not a destination as much as it is an evolving lifestyle.

It's something that progresses over time, and it increases as we continue to pursue intimacy with God and embrace who He created each of us to be.

I remember once worrying that I would be bored when I stopped entertaining and relying on the continual sexual fantasies that would go through my mind. Actually, I did go through a time that felt boring, but looking back it was due to the huge empty space in my heart and mind that was used to being filled with thoughts that would temporarily numb the longing in my soul to find fulfillment.

I knew God was showing me that Jesus needed to fill that place, but I was afraid I would find that to be unsatisfying. I felt guilty for being afraid that God wouldn't be enough. If God couldn't fill that place, I thought this meant I would either go back to the sin that had entrapped me for so long, or I would live a very empty and boring life with a permanent void in my heart.

Just the opposite happened though. What I didn't realize until later was that I was created for intimacy with Jesus. It's what I was made for. It's what you were made for as well.

I have found freedom in this area of my life, but I think sometimes the way we get there and what it looks like is different than we may expect. The lure that sexual temptation once had over me is not the same. It doesn't consume me. It doesn't take up space in my head and heart like it used to.

My temptations became less of an indicator of failure and more of an indicator of my continued need for intimacy with Jesus.

Some people assume since I am married that my husband fills the longing in my heart for intimacy. I did think marriage would satisfy that longing, but it only amplified that need. My husband was not designed to fill that place in my life, and I was not designed to fill that place in his life either.

Only Jesus can fill that deep need for intimacy.

While freedom and healing will look different for everyone, something I started to notice was that it reached out further than I thought it would. I saw changes coming to my marriage. They were not big or quick changes, but I could see them. I started being able to have more transparent friendships with other women. This was a direct and unexpected result of the healing taking place in my life. I started seeing that freedom and healing encompassed much more than I ever thought it would.

That may sound oversimplified, but I don't mean it to be.

During the process of addictions and/or habits being formed, at one point or another, we begin to realize that we cannot keep sexual sin in a box.

It affects every aspect of our lives.

Sexual strongholds affect our relationships, the way we see ourselves, the way we see others, our dating relationships, our marriages, our parenting journeys, and our relationship with God.

This is the same way healing and freedom works. There is so much more restoration ahead for you than *only* stopping your porn use, continual sexual fantasies, masturbation, and whatever else this stronghold entails for you.

This is not the endpoint for freedom and healing. It is just the beginning!

Just like sin has affected all aspects of your life, healing will affect all aspects of your life as well. Restoration, redemption, healing, and freedom will start to affect your relationships, friendships, the way you see yourself, the way you see others, your dating relationships, your marriage, your parenting journey, and your relationship with God.

Freedom from sexual strongholds is so much more than repenting from looking at porn, not fantasizing about someone, not masturbating, or not involving yourself in sinful relationships.

The areas that have been damaged due to our sin and brokenness are the same areas that can be transformed and redeemed when Jesus starts the process of healing our hearts and setting us free.

I pray this encourages you. Freedom and healing encompass so much more than stopping sinful behaviors. As God shows you any lies you have been believing that have kept you stuck and then shows you the truth, this will set you free. This is a continual process and only a part of the journey you will take as you continue to follow Jesus.

Reflection:

What has your definition of freedom from sexual strongholds been? Has it been helpful or harmful to you?

Action:

I mentioned in this chapter that the areas that have been damaged due to our sin and brokenness are the same areas that can be transformed and redeemed when Jesus starts the process of healing our hearts and setting us free.

Brainstorm and write down what you would like to see happen in your life outside of no longer being trapped in a sexual stronghold. What could your life look like? Pray and ask God to show you what your life could look like if you were set free from shame, and you had the kind of relationship with Him that you have always wanted? What would your other relationships look like? What would your heart look like?

11

Practicing Transparency

The more I learned how to open up to God about the very things I didn't want to talk about, the more I came up against a false idea that I had believed practically my entire life.

Deep down, I thought I should be fearful and nervous about telling Jesus what was going on in my heart. I fought the belief for quite some time that God is someone who wants me to do the right thing (focusing on my behavior) while pushing aside what's going on inside of me (my motives and heart issues).

I grew up in a home where good performance was especially praised. My dad was a teacher and it seemed that everyone in our community knew him. I learned how to blend in and behave myself in public. Even when my heart and thoughts did not match up, no one knew. I put an incredible emphasis on my behavior, not my heart.

I didn't know that what was going on inside of me was important. I thought everything just came down to making sure my actions were in line with what others expected of me. When they weren't in line, I had to make sure no one ever found out. This backfired on me later in life as I started to get involved in sexual relationships and later pornography. I had such a mess in my heart that I had ignored my whole life.

How many of us believe, on some level, that as long as we do what we're supposed to do, we get a checkmark from God? Especially when our heart is a mess, we feel like He doesn't want to hear what's going on with us on the inside.

We don't want a heart that feels broken, fractured, or toxic, but we often don't know that we have any other option but to try to hide or adapt to it.

As I talked about in an earlier chapter, it is wise to confide in trusted people in our lives. It's important to have someone in your life who will pray for you, give you wise counsel, and continually point you to Jesus. Sometimes, due to circumstances beyond your control, you may be unable to find that. Seasons of our lives can go by when we are left with no one around us to safely confide in or process everything with.

It is so important to know, whether we have someone else to talk to or not, we can take everything to Jesus. It's not easy but learning to be transparent with God is invaluable to our relationship with Him. He wants *all of you*, not just a fake person on the outside.

He knows the real importance of our hearts and wants us to express to Him what is going on with us on the inside. In doing this, He can show us lies we have been believing. He can reveal His truth to us regarding our situation.

He doesn't want an act.

He wants *all of you*.

There is power and healing that comes when we express to Jesus the deepest parts of our hearts.

Are you able to go before God and be transparent about the pain in your heart, sin, and even be willing to admit when your motivations regarding certain situations haven't been right? Going before Him in this way is always humbling and often scary when you are not used to it.

Psalm 62:8 says, "Trust in him at all times, O people; pour out your heart before him; God is a refuge for us. Selah."

Have you been able to be transparent with God in this way? We need to be able to go before Him concerning everything.

The very subject you feel you can't talk to Him about is the subject you need to talk to Him about. Learning to be transparent with Him can help set you free from the shame that often tries too hard to keep you quiet.

Part of practicing transparency with Jesus is having an awareness that He is with us always. We don't have to wait to go to a conference to pour our hearts out to Him and hear from Him. He is with us always.

Practicing transparency and hearing from Him doesn't need to start at a conference or a big event you are waiting for or sometime in the future when you have your life together. It begins at home doing your day-to-day activities. Practicing transparency begins when you are worrying about something during the day. This is something that can and should be part of your everyday life.

We all know the Holy Spirit is here with us, but when we have an awareness that He is truly here with us and waiting to talk with us, we will know that we don't have to wait for the big stuff to pour our hearts out to Him. Then when the big stuff comes, it won't be so excruciatingly difficult to talk to Him openly about it.

Start talking to Him about smaller situations first if you are struggling to talk to Him about your temptations or unwanted sexual behaviors. Make it a habit to talk to Him always.

I encourage you to start practicing transparency with Jesus if you haven't already. Talk to Him in the car. Do this out loud. Be transparent. Say the real stuff, not what you think you should say. He is waiting to build this kind of intimacy with you. Start with one sentence if you don't know how to say any more.

You may even find it easier to write it all down first. You can do this and read it out loud to Him when you are ready. This is how I started being transparent with God. It was just a little bit at a time.

Maybe you used to do this but stopped. Don't let guilt and condemnation continue to stand in the way. You can push past it and begin again. Pour your heart out to Him. Today is a good day to start! Pouring your heart out to Him will help clean out the junk in your heart.

Reflection:

Do you put on your best behavior around God and others, knowing that what's going on in your heart doesn't match?

Action:

Going before God and being transparent with Him is often scary when you are not used to it. It's also very humbling. Have you been able to do this yet? Write it down first, if you need to, and then read the paper out loud to Him. Little by little, it gets easier. He wants you to be transparent with Him. This is another way to build intimacy with Jesus. Don't forget to listen for His still, small voice when you are done.

12

When Porn Assaults Your Attractions

I could not write a book about sexual strongholds without including this chapter. This will not apply to all of you, but I know it will apply to many.

I have talked to many women over the years who are not attracted to women in real life and have no desire to be with one, yet they unexpectedly start feeling an attraction to the women they see in porn.

If this is something you are struggling with, this chapter is for you.

(If you are a woman who is wrestling with an attraction to women in real life and you're struggling with lustful thoughts you do not want, this is a huge part of my story. You may want to check out my first book, "Longing for Intimacy.")

If you have a physical and/or emotional response to women in porn, and not in real life, please know that this does not mean you are bi-sexual or a lesbian. Porn was created to evoke an emotional and physical response in everyone who watches it. It is designed to do this.

It can be difficult to navigate through this because we live in a society that is fixated on sexual identity. If you ask the world to make sense of these feelings and attractions, you will most likely conclude that you are bi-sexual or a lesbian.

Maybe you have no desire to physically act on these thoughts, but you are so confused about why seeing these women is suddenly so appealing to you. You may be feeling so fearful about this that your thoughts are a jumbled up mess over it all.

I want to break this down a little:

- Do you put yourself in the place of the women you see in porn?

- Do you imagine being desired in the same way?

- Do you wish you could look like the women you see in porn?

- Do you wish you had a deep connection (like the women in lesbian porn appear to have)?

- Do you wish you could have the same power that is portrayed in the scenes you have watched?

- Does the scene of two women together seem appealing to you because men are unsafe in your eyes?

I'm asking these questions, which is not an exhaustive list at all, because sometimes the attractions we can feel are a desire for something else. Please also realize that since pornography was created to stir up arousal, you are experiencing what the porn industry hoped you would feel.

Pornography warps everything God created as good.

It is a counterfeit substitute for the God-given desire we all have for love, intimacy, and connection. You have an enemy who would like nothing more than to heap confusion, shame, and fear on you to turn your focus away from Jesus. We must be so careful to guard our eyes and hearts. Watching porn opens people up to the enemy in a way that most people never knew could happen.

If you have been dealing with anything related to what I wrote about in this chapter, know that God is lovingly reminding you of who He made you to be. There is incredible life found when you embrace who He created you to be.

Maybe you are just now realizing that you have been believing lies straight from the enemy. I have found that when you mix situations like this with fear, they seem even more real (another trick of the enemy). Ask God to reveal to you the truth of who you are, and He will. If you ask Him to heal your heart, He will begin the process of doing so.

Hold on tightly to the truth and revelation He gives you. Write it down so you will have it later.

My prayer is that even after reading this chapter, some of you are being set free of the lies the enemy has been whispering in your ears. I believe blinders, confusion, fear, and deception are being removed so you can see the truth of who God says you really are.

This is all a process, but if you keep going you will find rest for your soul. You will be led into intimacy with the One who loves you, wants all of you, and treasures your heart more than anyone.

Reflection:

1. Have you considered how influential the porn industry is regarding the manipulation of your heart, mind, and body? Are you recognizing some of the lies they have convinced you of? What does God say about you instead?

Action:

If pornography has caused you to question your sexual identity, do you see yourself in any of the scenarios I listed above that may be helping to fuel this? If so, consider taking this to God and asking Him to show you the truth in this area.

Repent, renounce, and ask forgiveness for everything (porn, masturbation, erotic fantasies, etc.) you have participated in. Verbally break ties with all of it. Ask the Holy Spirit to remind you of anything you need to give to God. Lean on Him to renew your mind to see yourself as you were created to be.

(I will be talking in more detail about how to do this in Chapter 14.)

13

What Are Your Desires Telling You?

What comes to mind when you read the word *'desire?'*

Desires can show up in many ways in our lives. Certainly, some of them are good to have, but others we may recognize as being sinful or unhealthy. We can try to squelch them, but then they can pop back up again somewhere else.

Do you believe your desires are something good to have or are they something you need to restrain, ignore, or squelch?

For years I saw many of my desires as "bad" and something I needed to numb, ignore, or somehow squelch.

That didn't work.

I don't think it works for most of us.

Could your desires be telling you something different than you think?

From the very beginning of our lives, we were designed to connect with God and others. We were all created for connection, intimacy, and to be loved. We were also created as sexual beings, and this is something God created as good within the boundaries He has provided for us.

When we are wrestling with unwanted sexual behaviors such as pornography, lust, masturbation, sexual fantasies, or sexual affairs, it seems logical and like the right thing to look at our desires as something we need to either figure out how to cut off, give up, or extinguish in some way.

One woman may attempt to meet a desire to be loved by having a physical affair with someone, while another woman may attempt to meet her desire for connection by watching pornography or becoming emotionally attached to someone in an unhealthy way. Another woman may try to meet a desire to be loved by being a people pleaser.

Here is what I know:

Many of us have desires that are God-given, but we can sometimes try to fill them in unhealthy or sinful ways. This is one of the reasons that when we try to squelch our desires, they just pop up somewhere else.

When we attempt to meet our needs outside of God's design for us, this is where idols show up in our lives. An idol is anything or anyone we put above or before God.

Throughout the span of our lives, we have many opportunities to meet our desires (of all kinds, not just sexual ones) in ways that honor God, or we can attempt to meet our needs and fulfill our desires in selfish or sinful ways that separate us from Him.

Psalm 37:4 says, "Delight yourself in the Lord, and he will give you the desires of your heart."

Jesus wants to meet our desires! When we delight in Him, our hearts should begin to line up with Him and what He has for us.

- What desires have you had that have gone unmet?

- In what way(s) have you tried to meet those desires on your own?
- What do you crave?

I know for myself, I spent many years attempting to meet my desire for intimacy and connection with pornography and fantasizing about being with other women. I tried to stop and realized I couldn't stop so easily, so I decided that I should try to numb that desire.

I thought my desires for intimacy and connection were sinful.

I went back and forth between indulging in these desires and then trying to shut them down. What I didn't realize, though, was that these were God-given desires that could be met in healthy ways.

The roots of those desires were God-given.

When the Holy Spirit started showing me that the roots of those desires were God-given, this started a process of untangling my emotions and actions and releasing much of the shame that I was carrying. These desires were first met by building intimacy with Jesus, and then it flowed down to my husband and then my close friends. I used to persistently attempt to squelch something that is now being met in a way that honors God.

I didn't settle for anything. I gained so much more than I once thought I lost.

As I learned how to meet my desires in ways that honored God, I found that my desires were (and are) fulfilled much more often instead of feeling the continual pull and compulsion and drive for more.

Reflection:

Do you see any areas of repetitive sin in your life or strongholds that you may have been trying to numb or turn off?

Are there any desires that you have been trying to squelch, but they keep popping back up?

Could these desires in any way be connected to the love, intimacy, and connection you were created to have, or maybe another God-given need that you have?

Action:

How might you be able to meet those desires in a way that honors God? What is a small step you can take in that direction? I encourage you to journal about this, and you will be surprised what God will show you over time.

You don't need to dig for answers. (P*lease don't do this to yourself*.) The Holy Spirit can give you wisdom when you ask for it without you having to dig for it. He may not give you that wisdom today, but if you are open to hearing from Him, He will show you what you need to see in time.

14

Recognizing & Breaking Toxic Connections

Even after I eventually stopped watching porn, my thought life was out of control. My mind would drift off to sexual scenarios I had been a part of before, whether I wanted to do this or not. I began to realize that I did this all the time without even consciously thinking about it. I had also been having graphic sexual dreams for several years that would occur several nights a week.

Years into this, I learned about toxic ties that we can have with others. These toxic ties can be found in any kind of relationship. You may also hear this referred to as soul ties. Our souls consist of our mind, will, and emotions. These toxic connections involve our mind, will, and emotions.

The more I learned about soul ties, the more everything I was dealing with started to make sense.

From the very beginning, we were created to connect with our mother, father, and those closest to us.

We are created to connect with friends. 1 Samuel 18:1 says, "As soon as he had finished speaking to Saul, the soul of Jonathan was knit to the soul of David, and Jonathan loved him as his own soul."

For those of us who are married, we are also created to be knit together in this way with our spouse.

Genesis 2:24 says, "Therefore shall a man leave his father and his mother, and shall cleave unto his wife: and they shall be one flesh" (KJV). The word *cleave* means "to join." This is a spiritual act of being knit together.

There are also ties that we can form that are unhealthy and toxic.

Soul ties are often developed with parents, mentors or friends, authority figures, those whom we strongly admire, or with whom we have close or intimate relationships.

These kinds of relationships can form ungodly soul ties when the relationship is controlling or a "needy" relationship (codependent) where one person is very dependent on the other.

These are some indicators of having a toxic connection with someone:

- Being in a physically, emotionally, or spiritually abusive relationship but you feel too attached to cut off the connection even after trying repeatedly.

- You continue to think about the person long after the relationship or situation is over. You can't get them out of your mind.

- You have repetitive sexual dreams about someone from your past.

- When you do anything or make any kind of decision, you worry about what the other person will think of your decision. You worry if they will be angry or upset with you. You obsessively worry about another person, or someone else obsessively worries about you.

- Who do you feel controlled by?

- Do you have friends from way back that when you're around them you feel pulled back into the same sin as before?

- Have you bonded with someone or a group of people over gossip? Have you formed a negative bond with them in that way? Hint: Can you get together with them without gossiping about the same situation each time?

Toxic connections can also be formed when we have any kind of sexual contact outside of marriage:

1 Corinthians 6:16 says, "Or do you not know that he who is joined to a prostitute becomes one body with her? For, as it is written, 'The two will become one flesh.'"

Having sex outside of marriage causes us to bond with that person. It is a spiritual act just as much as a physical one. This is why there is no such thing as casual sex. Whether we realize it or not, our souls become joined to the other person.

I believe this can also happen with pornography. Our souls (mind, will, and emotions) are very much engaged in pornography use. Our souls connect with the people we see while we engage in masturbation. This is as much a spiritual act as it is a physical act.

This also applies to acts done against our will. Our souls are still involved just as much as our bodies. There is an ungodly connection that takes place. As I mention this, I want to quickly say that there is restoration available for all of us in this area.

These toxic ties can be broken, and Jesus can make us brand new. He can restore your sexuality just as He has been restoring mine.

What are some benefits of breaking this kind of toxic connection with others?

- This allows for restoration in our relationships.

- We can have restoration in our souls.

- Deliverance from sexual dreams and obsessive thoughts about someone.

- We will begin to experience freedom and wholeness in this area.

- Many times, a feeling of release from a person or situation will happen.

- This can often give us the ability to move on from people who once controlled us.

- Most importantly, it will allow us to walk more intimately with Jesus.

Reflection:

What are the toxic ties you need to break?

Sometimes it's a matter of not participating in certain activities that are not healthy for you. There may be people you need to stop hanging out with. It is important for you to pray about this and ask God to show you if there is anyone you need to move on from.

Something else that may be necessary is to remove certain contacts from your phone or on social media. Is there anyone on there who triggers you or who you know you should not be following or be friends with? You may need to move on from certain people. This is not easy, but it can be so crucial to continued healing in your life.

Action:

Come up with a plan of action regarding what you'll do next time you're put into a situation with a toxic co-worker, family member, or a person you have continually been tempted by or fallen into sin with.

Ask the Holy Spirit for help in doing this. He will lead the way for you.

Since these unhealthy ties are often also spiritual, something else you can do to break these ties is write down a list of the sexual activity you have been involved in outside of marriage. This would also include pornography or affairs inside or outside of marriage. If you cannot remember a name or never knew their name, you can include a short description of the person or situation instead. Write down a list of all you can remember.

When you are finished, pray something like this:

"Father God, please forgive me for these sexual activities: _____ with this person: _____. I repent for being involved in these sexual sins and activities, and I renounce the unholy connection I have had with them. Thank You for forgiving me and loving me the way You do. Please restore my mind, will, and emotions. In Jesus' name I pray. Amen."

If this was something that happened against your will, you can pray this:

"Father God, please release me from all ungodly ties with this person: _____ that happened due to this sexual activity: _____ that was committed against my will. I make the choice today to forgive them for what they have done to me. Thank You for loving me the way You do. Please restore my mind, will, and emotions. Please heal me from all the damage that happened to my heart and body as a result. In Jesus' name, I pray. Amen."

15

Equipped to Fight

"For our struggle is not against flesh and blood, but against the rulers, against the powers, against the world forces of this darkness, against the spiritual forces of wickedness in the heavenly places" Eph. 6:12.

As I have mentioned, fighting against sexual fantasies in my mind was a very long battle for me.

Later in my journey, the more I publicly shared my story, the more I was attacked by people who did not like what I was doing. I believe many of these attacks were designed by the enemy because I could not even count how many times I stumbled across porn (the exact same kind I used to look at) the day before I was supposed to speak somewhere. I talk a little bit more about this in the following chapter on rewiring our brain.

Whether your temptations involve men or women (or both), you are in a real spiritual battle.

I want to share with you one of the main ways I learned how to fight this spiritual battle. Whether you are battling pornography, masturbation, lust, or fantasizing (or all the above), God has not left you defenseless. He has already supplied you with what you need.

He shows us this in Ephesians 6:11-18 (AMPC):

"Put on God's whole armor [the armor of a heavy-armed soldier which God supplies], that you may be able successfully to stand up against [all] the strategies and the deceits of the devil.

"For we are not wrestling against flesh and blood [contending only with physical opponents], but against the despotisms, against the powers, against [the master spirits who are] the world rulers of this present darkness, against the spirit forces of wickedness in the heavenly (supernatural) sphere.

"Therefore put on God's complete armor, that you may be able to resist and stand your ground on the evil day [of danger], and, having done all [the crisis demands], to stand [firmly in your place].

"Stand therefore [hold your ground], having tightened the belt of truth around your loins and having put on the breastplate of integrity and of moral rectitude and right standing with God,

"And having shod your feet in preparation [to face the enemy with the firm-footed stability, the promptness, and the readiness produced by the good news] of the Gospel of peace.

"Lift up over all the {covering} shield of saving faith, upon which you can quench all the flaming missiles of the wicked [one].

"And take the helmet of salvation and the sword that the Spirit wields, which is the Word of God.

"Pray at all times (on every occasion, in every season) in the Spirit, with all [manner of] prayer and entreaty. To that end keep alert and watch with strong purpose and perseverance, interceding in behalf of all the saints (God's consecrated people)."

The armor of God is something God supplies for us to fight the battles we will face. This will help us to fight against all the strategies the enemy will use against us.

Darts will be fired at you, but God has given you armor to protect you. Have you been wearing your armor?

The enemy knows what has worked with you before. He will continue to tempt, discourage, anger, defeat you, and try what worked in the past, even if it seems to come to you in a new (but similar) way. Do not be fooled! Stand your ground and keep your eyes on the Lord.

If you fall, get back up and put your eyes back on Him again. Condemning yourself will only keep you down longer. Know who you are in Christ. Know who God created you to be, and don't let the enemy (through whatever means he uses) convince you otherwise. If you have given your life to Christ, you are a new creation.

Be aware of the tactics of the enemy but keep your focus on Jesus. Be aware of your surroundings. Listen to the Holy Spirit's voice. Pray at all times, in all seasons.

Develop a deep intimacy with Him. You will then begin to recognize the red flags He shows you along the way (before the enemy strikes) and the direction you should go when missiles are launched at you.

Fight with the armor the Lord has supplied for you. Renew your mind with His Word. He has given you the armor of a heavy-armed soldier so that you may be able to successfully stand up against the strategies of the devil.

2 Corinthians 10:5 says, "We are destroying speculations and every lofty thing raised up against the knowledge of God, and we are taking every thought captive to the obedience of Christ." It is so important to take every thought captive and not just dwell on every thought that comes into our minds.

Reflection:

Have you recognized that you are in a spiritual battle? How might your prayer life look different if you looked at this as a spiritual battle rather than purely a physical one?

Action:

Read Ephesians 6:11-18 again. Is there a specific part of God's armor that you could be using more often (belt of truth, breastplate of integrity, shield of faith, helmet of salvation, prayer, etc.)?

Think of an example of how you could apply that piece of God's armor in your life. Be equipped ahead of time, so you are ready for the battle before it begins.

16

Creating New Pathways

When we look at porn, masturbate, and repeatedly fantasize about sexual scenarios in our minds, our brains follow suit and start going in that direction automatically. When I realized this had happened to me, it scared me. I thought I had ruined my brain. It certainly felt like it! The porn I was looking at completely rewired my brain over time. I started to feel like I was looking at the world through a man's eyes and brain. It completely changed the way I saw both women and men.

This is part of the reason why it can be so incredibly difficult to stop. When I prayed to break the toxic connections I had, I still needed to renew my mind when I would run into temptations or when my mind would start to drift off into a direction it was used to taking all the time. I knew it would take time and perseverance to continue redirecting my thoughts.

When your brain gets used to you masturbating after thinking a certain thought or seeing a certain image, it starts going that way automatically. It directs itself along the path it has so easily been taking for so long. It's a well-traveled path, so taking a different route creates resistance. The good news is, with God's help we create new pathways in our brain.

It takes time and practice to reroute the path our brain is used to taking, but it is very possible to create new pathways in our brain. This doesn't just apply to this subject, but in any way that we need to renew our minds. The damage can absolutely be healed, and your brain can be restored.

As the Holy Spirit started revealing to me that my true need was intimacy with Jesus, this helped me to combat the temptations that would hit me. I want to give you another example of this from my own life, so you can see what helped me change my thinking and eventually re-route the direction my brain had been going for so long.

Whether your struggle with lust is with men or women, I pray this example from my own life below will be helpful for you. We can retrain our brains to see both men and women differently as Christ does.

I was at home one day finishing up a message I was preparing to share at a women's event the following morning. While taking a break, I checked my emails and was completely caught off guard when I scrolled down a little further to see an extremely graphic pornographic picture. This of course was the same kind of picture I searched for years ago. An array of emotions suddenly hit me, and I deleted the email as quickly as I could.

It's not like I hadn't accidentally come across any kind of porn before that day. I had. There were a few factors that lined up to hit the panic button for me this time though:

- I had an emotionally exhausting week.

- I was home alone that day. This was not normally a concern of mine at all, but suddenly it was fueling my fear.

- This picture was a perfect example of the kind I used to intentionally search for. It was like the enemy hand-picked it just for me.

I was frozen in fear, realizing that even though I deleted the email, I already could not get that picture out of my mind.

When I saw that picture, I felt a rush come over me that I hadn't felt in a very long time. Honestly, it terrified me. This was probably 5 years after I had stopped looking at porn. I forgot what that felt like, and I panicked. Shame washed all over me. I had just been preparing to share my testimony the following day in front of many people, and now I was being tempted to a degree I hadn't been tempted in a long time.

Then I realized something. I didn't have to listen to how I was feeling. I had the Holy Spirit to help me. I wasn't alone after all. He was there with me. I didn't have to listen to the shame that was telling me to hide. I started to pray, and I did something I had never done in the past.

I started praying for her.

I prayed for the woman in the picture I couldn't seem to get out of my head.

I prayed that God would give me eyes to see her the way He does. I prayed that the Lord would heal every wound in her heart and that she would give her life to Him. I prayed that the destiny God had planned for her life would be fulfilled. I prayed that God would release her from captivity and that she would share her story of healing and redemption with others.

To my surprise and relief, this worked.

The more I did this with temptations, the more I started to see women in the way God created me to see them. In addition, I started remembering to pray for protection before opening my email or social media.

Lusting after someone in my mind started to feel incredibly dishonoring, not gratifying.

I started learning that loving another woman meant that I would see her as God did and that I would want God's best for her.

I was determined to see other women as God does.

I would pray, *"Father God, help me to see her as You do. I pray that You show me who You created her to be. Give me eyes to see her just the way You do."*

I started to realize that if I truly valued other women, I was not going to lust after them. Loving another woman is helping her to see who God created her to be and *choosing to see her that way as well.* When we see people as God does, we will not lust after them.

Learning how to pray for women when I was tempted not only helped shift my focus away from what was going on in my mind and body, but it helped to refocus the way I saw them.

I praise God that I made a wise decision. The power that picture could have held over me was diminished when I continued to pray for her. I am so thankful that my relationship with God is not filled with so much shame anymore that I couldn't approach Him.

I encourage you to pray for the people you feel tempted by. If there's a man you're tempted to fantasize about, pray for him. Pray for him as you would a brother. Ask God to give you His eyes for him. This includes people you know and those on a screen. You can even do this for the people (real or not) who are in the sexual fantasies that run through your mind. He can restore the way you see others, so you start to see them as He does.

If you continually reroute your thinking, you can slowly rewire your brain.

You know your heart is in the process of being healed when lusting after someone starts to feel dishonoring, not gratifying. When we truly see men and women with the eyes of Jesus, we will want to care for their hearts by learning how to see them as He does.

All this needs to be done with God's help. We are responsible to do a measure on our own, but the process will not be complete without Jesus' help. If you need to be delivered from sexual dreams or compulsive behaviors, Jesus is your Deliverer. He can also help you renew your mind.

He can help you see both men and women differently. With His help, your brain can be healed and restored. Keep persevering! Do not give up. He can heal your heart and mind and set you free.

Reflection:

Have you ever prayed for the people you are tempted to fantasize about? (On a screen or in real life?)

Action:

Configure a list (ahead of time) of the ways you could pray for someone when tempted. Here are a few examples:

- Pray that God would let you see this person the way He does.

- Pray that the Lord would heal every wound in this person's heart.

- Pray that he/she would give his/her life to Jesus.

- Pray that the destiny God has planned for this person's life would be fulfilled.

- What else could you add here?

17

Who or What is Sustaining You?

"Behold, God is my helper; The Lord is the sustainer of my soul" Psalm 54:4 (NASB).

When I first started learning about finding sustenance in Jesus, I was afraid that looking to Jesus to sustain me (instead of pornography or my fantasies) would not work. I felt like I was wired differently and that these needs were truly sexual. How could Jesus possibly fill a need that I tried so hard to fill with porn and fantasy?

As I mentioned earlier, some of the deepest needs you have that seem related to sex may not actually have to do with sex.

The deep ache in your soul may seem filled up temporarily while fantasizing about someone and masturbating, but I don't have to convince you that this feeling doesn't last for very long. Sexual sin can come deceptively close to satisfying us, but it does not last.

Jesus is the only one who can sustain our souls.

Psalm 63:1-8 is an excellent example of what finding our sustenance in Jesus can look like:

"O God, you are my God; earnestly I seek you;
my soul thirsts for you;
my flesh faints for you,
as in a dry and weary land where
there is no water.
So I have looked upon you in the sanctuary,
beholding your power and glory.
Because your steadfast love is better than life,
my lips will praise you.
So I will bless you as long as I live;
in your name I will lift up my hands.

"My soul will be satisfied as with fat
and rich food,
and my mouth will praise you with joyful lips,
when I remember you upon my bed,
and meditate on you in the watches of the night;
for you have been my help,
and in the shadow of your wings

"I will sing for joy.
My soul clings to you;
Your right hand upholds me."

Finding sustenance in Jesus may be one of those topics you feel very far away from truly experiencing in your life. If so, you are in the right place! I have found that many Christians struggle with this. I most certainly did. I also need the occasional reminder to look to Him only for my sustenance. If I ever start to feel an incredibly empty feeling in the pit of my stomach that feels like it's consuming me, this is my red flag that I am probably looking to something or someone else other than Jesus to sustain me.

Sustenance means "life, nourishment, and livelihood." Do you find your means of life, nourishment, and means of livelihood in Jesus? If Jesus is the One who we are to look for to sustain us, how do we find this with Him?

Right now, each of us is being sustained by something or someone. We have looked to them to nourish us, to find life, and for our livelihood. Many of us have turned to sexual sin to comfort us while going back again and again.

For a time, it can feel like it is sustaining us. We continue to tell ourselves that if we just had *more,* it would finally sustain us. Sexual sin can feel like life for a time. What happens, though, is it leaves us feeling guilty, worn down, and empty. The more we go to these empty sexual behaviors for sustenance, the emptier we feel at the end of the day.

Who or what are you turning to for sustenance?

- Another person?
- A friend?
- A spouse?
- Porn?
- Fantasy?
- Masturbation?
- Food?
- Relationships?
- Sex?
- An emotional affair?
- Anything else?

Where do you turn when you are lonely?

Who or what do you turn to when you want to be comforted?

If we turn to sexual fantasies for sustenance, we will quickly find out when we try to stop fantasizing. If we turn to masturbation for comfort, we will quickly find out when we decide to stop.

Our flesh will scream at us when we stop doing something that was feeding it.

Certainly, it is not wrong to have people in our lives who support us and pray for us during difficult times. That is important for all of us to have. Our main source of nourishment, livelihood, comfort, and joy need to be found in Him. Otherwise, we are digging our own cisterns, so to speak.

Jeremiah 2:13 says, "for my people have committed two evils: they have forsaken me, the fountain of living waters, and hewed out cisterns for themselves, broken cisterns that can hold no water."

Cisterns hold water, and if we are striving to dig cisterns to sustain us, they will leak. They will have cracks we can't always see. The water we keep in these cisterns does not quench our thirst. We keep coming back to the same broken cistern unsatisfied because the water (sin) we have filled our cisterns with can never satisfy our body or our soul.

Jesus is the living water that sustains us. When we turn to anything other than Jesus to sustain us, we are forsaking our true source of living water.

The living water we have in Him will quench our thirst, unlike the water we gather for ourselves.

Reflection:

When we dig our own cisterns, they will leak. The water in them cannot quench our thirst. With what or whom are you trying to quench your thirst?

Action:

Pray and ask God to show you everything you have been attempting to find sustenance in. Are you ready and willing to surrender anything or anyone whom you have been trying to find sustenance in outside of Jesus?

18

Surrender

Every time I continued fantasizing about certain scenarios in my mind, I was destroying any hint of intimacy that my husband and I had. I thought my only opportunity to have a deep connection with someone again would mean being with another woman. As a result, I was destroying my marriage from the inside out.

As I started learning how to build intimacy with Jesus, I would find that the fantasies and temptations I wrestled with would all come rushing back when I started going through difficult times in my life.

The Holy Spirit started showing me very clearly that I had been idolizing women. I wasn't just putting my desires above my marriage, but I was putting them above God.

This is when I started to see the state of my own heart. I knew what I was doing was sinful but looking back I chose to do it because I thought it was a need I had that wasn't being met. I thought my only chance at happiness was to be with another woman, but I knew I couldn't have that. I needed to lay that desire down at Jesus' feet.

I started to see that I was willing to compromise so many things to have what I felt like I so badly desired.

God started showing me that I needed to surrender my heart's desires over to Him. I needed to surrender to Him what I felt I was entitled to have but wasn't allowed to have.

Letting go felt like I was letting go of a piece of my own heart. Even more so, it felt like a part of my heart was being ripped out.

I will be very honest with you. As I attempted to surrender this huge idol in my heart, it was painful, scary, and humbling. It was something I was very attached to. It felt like I was laying down my only chance to be happy (even though the porn and fantasies were never enough, and I knew it).

This deeper place of healing He was taking me through was intense and painful, but it amazed me how much peace I would have when I stopped digging for answers all the time and just waited on the Holy Spirit for direction.

I had asked for forgiveness before, but this felt different. It *was* different.

We can sometimes hope He will swoop in and fill that place so we can then let go of our idols, but that's often not how it works. We need to take the scary step of letting go of our idols (no matter what they are) first, and then Jesus can take His rightful place in our hearts and lives.

Have you surrendered your heart's desires, temptations, and fantasies to Jesus?

Is there anything that you need to let go of that has been in the way of your relationship with Him?

Recognizing that we may need to lay down an idol (no matter what subject it is related to) can be scary and painful, but there is so much hope, freedom, fulfillment, and intimacy with Jesus to be gained as a result.

He doesn't ask us to lay all of this down because He doesn't care about our desires or dreams. He asks us to lay them down to draw us in closer to Him and to refine us. At the same time, He refines our heart's desires and dreams.

I have gained so much more than I have lost since I allowed Jesus to take the place that only He should have in my heart. I didn't trade idols and put my husband there (although I tried that too).

Only Jesus can fill that place in my heart.

Only Jesus can fill that place in *your* heart.

Reflection:

Has porn, fantasy, lust, or another person filled a place in your heart that should never be?

I completely get it. It can be very difficult, scary, and painful to let go. You may want to let go of your idols or dreams but not know who you are without them. The comfort it all provides can be alluring, but if it's not something Jesus has for you, it is a form of false intimacy and will prevent you from experiencing the true intimacy that you were meant to have with Jesus.

Action:

This is something you can pray:

"Lord, I pray that You reveal to me any idols I have been worshipping, knowingly or unknowingly. Please forgive me for worshipping anything/anyone besides You. I choose to turn away from these idols. In response, I turn to You, the only One worthy of my worship. Fill these places in me that I have tried to fill with other things/people. I break all ungodly connections with these idols, in Jesus' name. Thank You for loving me enough to show me what's in my heart. It's not to condemn me, but to heal and restore me. It's so I can draw closer to You. Show me who the Holy Spirit is. I want to know Him better. Show me what intimacy with You is. In Jesus' name, I pray. Amen."

19

A Time to Grieve

Surrendering our fantasies, hopes, and dreams to Jesus can be painful. I know and understand the grief, pain, and grieving process that can go along with the decision to let go and fully surrender this to Jesus. Even when we don't want it anymore and we know it's hurting us, it can be painful to let go.

Laying down the sinful habits that have been comforting us can also be very challenging. We can go through a grieving process, even in letting go of sin. Sexual sin often seems to comfort us. It can be easy to not want it but not know what life is like without it.

Comfort and familiarity can seem less scary than the pain of surrender.

In the Bible there are many times David pours his heart out to God. When experiencing deep pain, this is an excellent opportunity to practice transparency with God. In Psalm 13 (NASB), David transparently pours his heart to Him in this way:

"How long, LORD? Will you forget me forever?
How long will you hide your face from me?
How long am I to feel anxious in my soul,
With grief in my heart all the day?
How long will my enemy be exalted over me?

"Consider and answer me, O LORD my God;
Enlighten my eyes, or I will sleep
the sleep of death,
And my enemy will say, 'I have overcome him,'
And my adversaries will rejoice
when I am shaken.

"But I have trusted in your faithfulness;
My heart shall rejoice in your salvation.
I will sing to the LORD,
Because He has looked after me."

When I surrendered my heart and desires to Jesus, I went through a deep time of grieving. At the time, I didn't know if grieving was something

I should even do because much of it was surrounding what God didn't want for me.

This is when I started learning about the Holy Spirit being my Comforter. As I started embracing this, I realized He wanted me to take this grief to Him. He wasn't angry with me for feeling it, and He didn't want me to shove it down or pretend it wasn't there.

I have kept a journal for many years, and I want to share with you something I wrote when I surrendered my heart's desires to Jesus and was grieving.

Letting Go

"I am choosing to forgive you.
I am choosing to forgive myself.
I think I am now finally able to let go
of all of the things I cannot change.

"I am letting go of the dreams
my heart felt that were so real,
yet so destructive and poisonous
to my soul.

"I am letting go of the lie
that I can find true intimacy with you.
I idolized you and put you in a place
that you were never meant to fill.

"I gave you a power over my life
that you didn't even want.
A power over my life that only
God should have, and for that I am sorry.

"My heart is letting go of the hope
of finding true closeness
in a relationship that can
ultimately only bring death.

"I am letting go
so God can take His rightful place
in my heart and in my life
so healing can begin
and life can begin to bloom in my heart.

"I feel grieved over this
but it's mostly a grief that comes from
trusting in something for so long
that can never come to pass,
for trusting the deception thrown at my heart.

"I release all of this to You,
Father God, my Savior, my Redeemer,
The Author of my life and all of my days.
I know that You forgive me and only want
my heart to be healed, whole, happy, and joyful.

"My heart is starting to feel again.
It is scary to let go.
But I trust You, Lord.

"You are my true Protector,
and I know You are leading me
towards the freedom I've always searched for.

"Thank You for never letting me go.
Thank You for never giving up on me.
Thank You for never forgetting about me.
Thank You for showing me the LIFE found in You.

"I have released all of this into Your hands.
My hands and heart have let go,
and I will never turn back.
My eyes are fixed on You."

That painful time of my life ended up being a very sweet time in my life as I began to embrace the Holy Spirit as my Comforter. As strange as it seems, if it wasn't for this pain and suffering, I would never have had the opportunity to know the comfort of the Holy Spirit.

No one wants pain. It can be excruciating. We never know how long it will last. When we are misunderstood or hurried through it by others, it can be especially difficult.

When we are in the middle of it, though, we have the opportunity to know the comfort of the Holy Spirit in a way we could have never known otherwise.

Laying down the idols that comforted me was something I needed to do first. Then I felt the pain and grief of that seemingly huge absence from my life. Like I said in the last chapter, it felt like I had let go of a piece of my own heart.

As I laid it all down and asked the Holy Spirit to take the place of everything I was using to comfort me, He started comforting me in a way only He could. I started seeing, more and more, that the times I was tempted to fantasize the most was when I was craving a deep connection with someone and when I was seeking comfort. Again, it came back to continuing to build intimacy with God and seeking comfort from the Holy Spirit.

I remember finally realizing that I had been seeking comfort from those fantasies for so long when the Holy Spirit was right there wanting to comfort me all along.

I remember feeling uncomfortable relying on Him so much at first. I had always fought the need to be overdependent on the relationships I had, and I started to feel needy when it came to the Holy Spirit after I started relying on Him more and more. God showed me that I was created to rely on Him. It was not wrong or needy, and it was not the same thing as relying on people too much or being in a codependent relationship with someone.

Reflection:

Do you know the Holy Spirit as your Comforter?

If you surrender your heart's desires, fantasies, dreams, and idols to Jesus and then feel the pain of that loss, you can ask the Holy Spirit to take His rightful place and be your Comforter. He is the best comforter there is. There is often a gap of time in between letting go of something and the comfort we feel. That empty gap of loneliness may feel terrible, but it shows us how much we were depending on something other than God to fill us. He will fill that place in due time. If you feel that deep ache of emptiness in the gap in between, keep persevering! God will fill that place, and it will one day be sweeter than before.

Action:

Don't be afraid to grieve if you need to grieve. It's not a sign of weakness or a lack of faith. The pain that comes from surrendering your desires, fantasies, and idols to Jesus does not at all compare to the joy that comes later. That may sound far-fetched right now. Remember, Jesus wants *all of you*.

Be honest about your reservations. There is no such thing as relying on Him too much. He is your perfect comforter in times of pain and grief.

If it would help, write a poem like I did or just words that will help express how you are feeling. You may not even know how you are feeling until you start to write it down. Read this out loud to God.

Remember, He is your comforter. He won't push you away or roll His eyes at your pain. He wants to comfort you. It is ok and very healthy to grieve.

20

Maintaining Your Healing Journey

Freedom is an ongoing process. Just like intimacy with Jesus, freedom is continual and must be maintained.

It is so important to take care of ourselves physically, emotionally, mentally, and spiritually. When we are tired, stressed, weary, or not feeling well, we can be more vulnerable to the lure of temptation. You know this as well as I do.

Many of us learned to turn to masturbation, fantasy, or porn for stress relief. It is wonderful to break free from sinful or destructive habits, but we also need to replace them with something else. This will take time, practice, and perseverance.

I am including a few suggestions below that will be important for you to continue on the path of freedom and healing and to continue growing in your relationship with Jesus:

Focus on healthy relationships and boundaries

It's so important to set boundaries and to focus on healthy relationships. Toxic relationships can be extremely draining, and it is healthy to set boundaries where they are needed. Who energizes you, inspires you, and continually points you to Jesus? This is who you need to spend your time with.

Is there someone in your life (a friend, someone you are dating, or an ex) who you know is not healthy to be around? Maybe you find that you get caught up in fantasy or sexual sin when you are with them or after you spend time with them. This is not healthy for you and being with them will prohibit your healing process.

Be mindful of how social media is affecting you

Pay attention to how social media is making you feel. It can be extremely beneficial to hide posts or people who drain your energy and to take regular breaks from social media. I often don't realize how much I need it until I take a break for a while.

Exercise and eat healthy

You may be wondering why I included this. It is not a misprint. When we exercise and eat healthy food, we feel so much better. This has been a game changer for me. As I started walking a few days a week, stopped eating most processed foods, and stopped eating sugar (except for certain kinds of fruit), my joints stopped aching. I feel so much better, and my mind is much clearer when I eat this way. It is then easier for me to pray, read my bible, and do anything else during my day that takes concentration. It's easier to resist temptation and make wise choices when we are feeling healthy and clear-minded. Don't forget to drink water!

Set aside time to get enough sleep and rest

Good sleep is vital for your health. Quiet time is beneficial for everyone, especially if you are wired as an introvert like I am. I realize there are seasons in our lives when getting enough sleep and rest is very challenging. Do the best you can in the particular season you are in.

Connect with others regularly

The more I connect with others who encourage me, who I can bounce ideas and thoughts off of, who I can be transparent with, and who can do the same with me, the better I feel. So much healing can take place in community. If you do not have a solid Bible-believing church you are a part of, pray about where you can go and get connected with other believers. This is so important.

Be kind to yourself

As you implement what you have learned in this book and what the Holy Spirit has spoken to you, please be patient with yourself. This is not an overnight process. It's often the small and steady changes we continue to make over time that make the biggest difference in our lives.

Make sure there is a safe person in your life who you can be real and transparent with. It's also okay to say "no" if you are overwhelmed. This is also part of setting boundaries and being kind to yourself.

Remember to treat yourself with care and to continue building intimacy with Jesus. Continue practicing taking everything to Him and listen for His response. You will want to maintain this close relationship with Jesus when everything is going well.

When trials hit you will already be close to Him. If you mess up, ask God to forgive you. Try not to condemn yourself. This will only make things worse. Turn to Jesus instead. He is not condemning you but wants you to come to Him with what happened. This is the only way to get your heart right with Him again. Get back up as quickly as possible and start back on the path Jesus is leading you on. He is with you.

Stay close to Jesus during wilderness seasons

There was a time in my life after I had already been publicly sharing my testimony for a couple of years when I found myself starting to get *very* restless and frustrated. I was finding myself suddenly tempted in ways that I had not been tempted in a long time. I started feeling so weary. I couldn't think of anything I did to cause this to happen, and I had no idea what was going on. This was also after a prolonged time of healing in my life.

The worst part was, God seemed silent.

Old temptations were resurfacing, and it felt like I lost all the ground I had worked so hard to gain. I was convinced I was going backwards. This seemed to happen out of nowhere. Where I had learned to be content, I suddenly felt extremely discontent. Lies I had stopped believing about myself and God were suddenly seeming very real again. It felt like God abandoned me. All the progress I made seemed to be slipping out of my hands, and it scared me. I didn't know of anything I did to make this happen.

I didn't realize it at the time, but I was in a wilderness season.

We all go through seasons of testing and wilderness seasons where God seems silent. One way I have discovered to find refuge during times like this is to abide in the secret place. This is a place of rest, safety, shelter, and intimacy with God. I will talk about that more in the final chapter.

Galatians 6:9, "And let us not grow weary of doing good, for in due season we will reap, if we do not give up."

Isaiah 40:31, "but they who wait for the LORD shall renew their strength; they shall mount up with wings like eagles; they shall run and not be weary; they shall walk and not faint."

Don't give up in wilderness seasons. God prunes those who are His. Keep your eyes on Him. He has not left you. You have not lost all you worked so hard for. Freedom is real. Keep your focus on Him and do what you know you need to do, and dwell with Him in the secret place. He is with you. You will come out the other side stronger, having deeper intimacy with Him if you continue to follow Him.

Reflection:

Have you been taking care of yourself physically, emotionally, mentally, and spiritually?

Action:

What is one change you can start with to take care of yourself and maintain your healing journey?

Find and write down a scripture you can stand on while you are trusting Jesus to heal, deliver, and restore you.

21

Dwelling in the Secret Place

I saved this chapter for the end of the book very intentionally. Dwelling in the secret place is vital to our walk with God. One of the most important things you and I can do is begin our day with Jesus and keep our eyes on Him throughout the day. We need to learn how to abide in the secret place. There are many different places in the bible where dwelling in the secret place is mentioned. To *dwell* somewhere means "to live or stay there as a resident."

If we dwell in the secret place, this means we are to live there. This is a place of shelter, safety, and refuge. In the secret place, we make ourselves more vulnerable before God and experience His intimate love for us.

Prayer, reading scripture, and quiet time with Jesus are all vital to our relationship with Him. The secret place is not a physical place but more of a posture of our hearts. It's a place of shutting out the world around us and getting alone with Him.

It is vital for your continued healing and freedom to dwell here. Even more than this it is vital for your relationship with Jesus. It's in the secret place where we are changed. Do you need a place of safety or refuge? This is the secret place.

Psalm 91:1-16 (NKJV)

"He who dwells in the secret place
of the Most High
Shall abide under the shadow of the Almighty.
I will say of the LORD, 'He is my
refuge and my fortress;
My God, in Him I will trust.'

"Surely He shall deliver you from
the snare of the fowler
And from the perilous pestilence.
He shall cover you with His feathers,
And under His wings you shall take refuge;
His truth shall be your shield and buckler.

"You shall not be afraid of the terror by night,
Nor of the arrow that flies by day,

"Nor of the pestilence that walks in darkness,
Nor of the destruction that lays
waste at noonday.
A thousand may fall at your side,
And ten thousand at your right hand;
But it shall not come near you.

"Only with your eyes shall you look,
And see the reward of the wicked.
Because you have made the LORD,
who is my refuge,
Even the Most High, your dwelling place,
No evil shall befall you,
Nor shall any plague come near your dwelling;
For He shall give His angels charge over you,
To keep you in all your ways.

"In their hands they shall bear you up,
Lest you ⌈dash your foot against a stone.
You shall tread upon the lion and the cobra,
The young lion and the serpent you shall trample
underfoot.

"'Because he has set his love upon Me,
therefore I will deliver him;
I will ⌈set him on high, because he has
known My name.
He shall call upon Me, and I will answer him;
I will be with him in trouble;
I will deliver him and honor him.

"With long life I will satisfy him,
And show him My salvation.'"

Do you have a quiet place where you meet with God? I realize we are all in different seasons in our lives. My alone time with God looks very different than it did when my children were toddlers. The time I set aside every day to spend time with Him is first thing in the morning because that's what works best for me.

Something that helps me is to keep a notebook beside me when I am spending alone time with God. This has two purposes. I can write down what the Holy Spirit speaks to me or something that stands out to me. Also, I use this to write down anything that comes to my mind that I forgot to do or need to do. That way, I can get it off my mind and turn my attention back to God, knowing it will be there for me to see later.

What happens when we are tempted when out in public or having a trying time at work? Does that mean we have to wait until we get back home to get into the secret place again? No. This can take more practice, but it is possible to enter into the secret place when in a room filled with people or even in the grocery store. This is how we can live there.

It is possible to quiet our minds and hearts and to turn our attention to God in a room filled with people. It's a heart posture. We need to listen for His still, small voice. It would be great practice to try this daily. The next time you are out in public, try turning your attention to Jesus and listening for the Holy Spirit's whisper.

I encourage you to practice this. Once you learn how to discipline your mind and heart to do this, you will be able to do it anytime. This will come in very handy later, especially when you need to access the secret place quickly.

The secret place with God is where you are transformed, renewed, refreshed, and where you will find life. Our source of hope and life is in Jesus, and in Him alone.

I don't believe there can be true freedom from sexual strongholds without having a relationship with Jesus. If you made it to the end of this book and still haven't given your life to Jesus, I encourage you to do that now. He desires to be your Lord and your Savior.

The sins we commit (all of them – not just the sexual ones) separate us from God. The punishment for your sin and my sin is death. Your sin must be paid for to go to Heaven. Jesus paid for your sin on the cross. He did this so you would not have to go to hell and so you could live with God forever.

You cannot earn this. It's a gift from Him. That's what's so beautiful about all of this. It's a gift! Giving your life to Him and making the decision to be faithful to Him is vital. It's the most important decision you will ever make.

Ask Him for forgiveness of your sins and to be your Lord and Savior. Ask Him to guide you and teach you, and He will.

Reflection:

Distractions and shame can keep us from entering into the secret place. Guilt can also prevent us from feeling like we can be in His presence. Sometimes even feeling overwhelmed with not knowing how to spend this quiet time with God can keep us from doing this.

Have you been abiding in the secret place? Why or why not?

Action:

If you haven't been abiding in the secret place, what are some practical steps you can take to start practicing this?

Conclusion

I am praying that what I have written in this book has helped equip you in your journey of seeking freedom from sexual strongholds. This is all a process! I believe much of it will help you in many other areas of your life as well.

I also hope it challenged you to know that you can trust Jesus with your entire heart.

I pray that you begin to experience freedom in many different areas of your life as you continue walking out your healing journey. Jesus is your healer, deliverer, helper, restorer, redeemer, and your guide.

He loves you, and He wants *all of you*.

Amy

30904048R00095